FIGHTING BUDDHA

Martial Arts, Buddhism, Kicking Ass and Saving It

FIGHTING BUDDHA

Martial Arts, Buddhism, Kicking Ass and Saving It

JEFF EISENBERG

FINDHORN PRESS

© Jeff Eisenberg, 2017

The right of Jeff Eisenberg, to be identified as the author of
this work has been asserted by him in accordance with the Copyright,
Designs and Patents Act 1998.

Published in 2017 by Findhorn Press, Scotland

ISBN 978-1-84409-722-7

A CIP record for this title is available from the British Library.

Cover Photo by Richard Crookes
Author photo by Alix Petricek

Edited by Nicky Leach
Cover design by Richard Crookes
Interior design by Damian Keenan
Printed and bound in the USA

Published by
Findhorn Press
117-121 High Street,
Forres IV36 1AB,
Scotland, UK

t +44 (0)1309 690582
f +44 (0)131 777 2711
e info@findhornpress.com
www.findhornpress.com

Contents

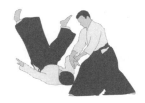

FOREWORD

Like the author, one of my earliest childhood memories is of the Sunday ritual of watching kung-fu films with my father. I would flip-flop between watching intently and jumping about in the living room, mimicking the movements of the actors on the television. The sights and sounds of the martial arts mythical superheroes captivated my senses, while appealing to my enjoyment of the fantastic.

Because my father taught martial arts, I knew that it was a different story in the dojo. The movies were fake at best, blasphemous at worst, and my father always sternly made that clear. He often casually mocked showmanship, fancy body movements, and ultra-high kicks. He would tell me, "Shawn, I don't need to be able to kick above your knee to completely immobilize you. I can simply break your knee." His approach was minimalistic, coupled with Eastern philosophical musings.

I was taught that the martial arts are a lifelong journey to gain better understanding of ourselves and the world around us. In conjunction with this philosophy, I was also taught the tools for self-defense. Training at the dojo took up a good amount of time during my childhood. It was something I enjoyed, yet full-on sparring was brutal at times. I hadn't yet developed a tolerance for pain, which created fear and a desire to avoid the walls of the dojo.

I discovered skateboarding around the same time, which only helped accelerate my declining interest in the martial arts. Not long after being led to an abandoned and empty pool by my older cousin, where we could practice skateboarding, I found myself telling my father that I no longer wanted to train at the dojo; I wanted to focus on skateboarding. My father was upset, and as a father myself now, I can understand that pain. But it was time for me to step out from his shadow and push forward on my own path.

Soon after I fully dedicated myself to skateboarding I also started surfing. I enjoyed both, as they required my full focus and helped clear my increasingly turbulent mind, but surfing touched deeper elements inside me, creating an intimate bond with the ocean and nature.

At the time, I didn't understand that the joy I derived from these seemingly frivolous activities came as a result of being fully present in the moment. The same presence required of me in sparring—the same presence I ran away from—I now found myself experiencing in critical moments on the transitioned walls of the pool or upon the face of an open wave. It was while immersed in these crucial moments that I was finding both my peace and my joy.

"Presence," "present moment," and "awareness" are words we now hear often in our cultural lexicon in the West. Yet we may experience these states of being in different ways. For the martial artist, it may be found in the fire of a heated moment of altercation; for the surfer, it may come as a result of dropping into a large wave that will swiftly stand up vertical on the shallow sandbar beneath the water's surface. In each case, the situation calls upon clarity of mind and supreme focus.

It was over fresh organic juices and discussions on presence in extremely consequential situations that my friendship with Jeff Eisenberg was born. I was running a small vegan café and juice bar in downtown Asbury Park, New Jersey, where Jeff and his wife were regulars. The café was coupled with a yoga studio, and I taught group surf lessons to all the yogis in town.

One summer's morning, I took Jeff and his wife surfing, next to one of the numerous jetties that reach into the ocean from the coastline. Sometimes, depending on the student, surf lessons can become a discussion in philosophy and appreciating being with nature. The first half of the session went like this, until the tide dropped enough for the waves to break safely away from the shoreline. Then, after a few attempts at catching a wave, Jeff momentarily got to his feet on the board and found himself experiencing that similar presence he felt while engaged in martial arts.

Afterwards, we spoke about how there can be nothing else in those heavily demanding moments—that an uninterrupted, calm mental state is a requirement for success. I enjoyed the talk, as I fancied myself a student of martial arts philosophy and found myself applying it to my surfing.

As our discussion continued, Jeff expressed the view that philosophy and practice are nearly useless if they are never applied in a real-life situation. For me, this may mean charging into a ferociously large wave; in Jeff's case, it may manifest as facing an opponent on the mat or in the street. In either situation, routine and mechanics are set aside as spontaneity and intuitive flow are called upon. Knowledge must become wisdom through action. This is true on the mat, in the street, in our heads, and among the waves.

Having dedicated decades to the martial arts and Buddhist practice, Jeff Eisenberg has gained experiential knowledge of the successes and pitfalls of both paths. As he explains in this book, to be present in the here and now, opening to the eternal moment, by way of our path of choice, even when faced with chaotic situations, this is the spirit of the Fighting Buddha. Read on, and partake of this humble offering of spirit.

Peace and Blessings,
Shawn Zappo
Meditation teacher, surfing instructor, father, and writer
www.surfandabide.com
January, 2017

PREFACE

Fighting Buddha is a memoir that details my 40-plus-years' journey in martial arts and meditation training and 25 years of Buddhist practice. Using autobiographical anecdotes, along with martial art fighting strategies, Buddhist folk stories, and koan and sutra teachings, it explores both the benefits and detriments of each practice, as well as how they complement each other as a singular practice.

My intention in writing this book was to provide Buddhist practitioners with martial arts fighting strategies that support a realistic application of the Buddha's teachings, to show martial artists how they could utilize Buddhist concepts in the development of the mental discipline needed for technique application, and to articulate to practitioners of both disciplines what to look for and avoid in both practices, using examples drawn from my own experiences.

This is not to say that I'm proposing that my way is the only way, or the best way; nor is it my intention to cast any Buddhist practice or martial art in a negative light. On the contrary, my objective was to present a truthful, albeit sometimes critical look at Buddhism and martial arts as they pertain to the evolution of my own Buddhist practice and martial arts training. I hope to help other practitioners with similar goals avoid the mistakes I have made and avoid wasting the time I have wasted.

The general premise of this book is that martial arts techniques done in the controlled environment of the dojo and meditative experiences that depend on the environment of the zendo for their effectiveness will never have an appropriate application unless trained, practiced, and tested under real-life circumstances. For the martial artist, this prompts the question of whether traditional training in the dojo can actually be utilized in a real situation, and for the Buddhist practitioner, whether the rituals, scholarly study, and meditative experience of the zendo can translate into skillful action outside it.

These issues are not semantics or hyperbole. They are the result of my experiences as a bodyguard and as the director of crisis response in the emergency room and psychiatric ward of a major hospital, where in both instances, I quickly came to the sad realization that most of what I had learned and thought applicable over many years of martial arts training was not. Likewise, I had a similar experience when I found that much of what I was focusing on in my Buddhist studies had little bearing on how I was actually living. In both instances, this was not due to a lack of effort but rather, due to inadequate material that failed my effort.

These questions are a running theme throughout this book, in which I address the struggles of beginning martial arts training and Buddhist practice, the importance of identifying goals and choosing a teacher and training in support of them, and most importantly, how to determine whether the training can be assimilated into real-life application.

Prior books have been written about martial arts and spiritual practice, but what makes my book completely different is that other books focus on only the "art" or practice aspect and not the "martial" or realistic application of martial arts. A common belief about martial arts that has become synonymous with spiritual practice is that only the "soft" styles—those trained slowly with a mandate that they never actually be used—can be considered meditative practice, while "hard" styles, which emphasize fighting, are not only non-conducive to meditative practice but are nothing more than mindless violence.

I address these assumptions in the following ways: by discussing the difference between violence and the use of martial arts as it relates to the Buddha's teaching of "cause no harm"; by exploring the common misunderstanding that meditative moments are exclusive to only select activities; and by explaining why the true test of a martial artist's skill and of a Buddhist's application of mindfulness is during a situation that is least conducive to it.

Building upon this discussion, I then describe how I myself apply Buddhist teachings in my own daily life. I conclude the book by offering definitions of enlightenment and the black belt and correcting common misconceptions about them, i.e., that they are not the end results of one's practice but the beginning.

As this is a book about my modern take on practicing ancient teachings, I'm aware that my writing style and tone at times does not fit the common perception of how a "Buddhist" or "martial arts master" sounds. But to be anything other than true to myself in the way I write would contradict the central message of this book. Sometimes irreverence and rebellion are needed in order to sharpen the sword and cut through delusion. I hope my use of humor and self-deprecation tempers that blade enough to show that I unsheathe it motivated only by compassion, in a quest to "save all beings."

In closing I'd like to remind the reader that in his time, the Buddha was the most radical, anti-establishment progressive the world had ever seen. My intention in writing this book is that in some small way, I am keeping his spirit alive!

Jeff Eisenberg
Jersey Shore, New Jersey
January, 2017

INTRODUCTION

It's not a perfect world ...
and it's not, not a perfect world

I was once teaching self-defense to a class of 10-year-olds and pointed out how important it is for the martial arts student to understand that training is merely preparation for reality, and not reality itself. My point was that scenarios practiced in the dojo will never go the same way twice in the street. I then demonstrated a technique and said, "Remember, it will go this way in a perfect world, but realistically, we must be prepared to do it many different ways since it isn't a perfect world."

As I began to demonstrate an alternative application of a technique, my young student Henry raised his hand. "Sir," he said, with his trademark seriousness and unwavering conviction, "realistically, in a perfect world, we wouldn't *need* to protect ourselves."

He was right. In a perfect world there would be no need to train, no need to protect ourselves, no need for dharma practice, no need to liberate ourselves. But it isn't a perfect world, and here lies the root of our suffering. Our struggle is that we are drawn to martial arts training and Buddhist practice, thinking that we can create our perfect world. We mistakenly think that the result of our work will be the elimination of experiences that cause us pain and suffering rather than understanding that practice and training teach us to develop new skills and strategies for when we *have* painful experiences.

Martial arts students think they will reach some special, high level of training that will make them invincible fighting machines that are always safe. Buddhist newbies think that they will reach some special, high level of practice that will give them a state of permanent bliss. The truth is that the best a martial artist can hope for is to be able to assess and evacuate a threat scenario and, at worst, to survive it with the least amount of injury. The best a dharma practitioner can hope for is to respond to painful experiences with new, helpful behavior that is free of attachment, and at worst, break attachment and not turn pain into suffering.

Practice and training should turn us toward these realizations and have us face and accept them. If they turn us away from these truths, then we are wasting our time with harmful delusion. Not to sound like a crazy Zen master, but the world isn't perfect, but it is also not ... *not* perfect.

We must accept things just as they are and deal with them! There will always be a scary dude in the shadows waiting to kick our ass, and life will never, *ever* go exactly the way we think it should! So we must train as though every day *is* the day that we will come face to face with that scary dude in the shadows, and we must practice the dharma every day as though everything that *can* go wrong *will!*

1

THE FUNNY-LOOKING FAT GUY

I am not a god; I am awake.
— BUDDHA

My first contact with the Buddha was as a kid. He was everywhere. There were statues in the house, outside in the garden, and my mother always seemed to paint them in her paintings, which hung throughout the house. Even a lot of the furnishings had an Eastern flair.

Before you start forming an image of a little flower child growing up in the Buddhist home of a hippie painter up near Woodstock in the beautiful Catskill Mountains, or in some northern California commune, I must tell you that the truth is much weirder than that. The reality is that I grew up in Jersey, right outside of New York City, and to top it off, we weren't even Buddhist!

In fact, in spite of all the Buddhist imagery around, I never remember hearing anything about him, nor was any of that imagery ever discussed. I know you're probably saying to yourself, "Okay, they weren't Buddhists, but they were probably just into meditation." Wrong! Medication, yes; meditation, no!

So I decided that all the statues and pictures of the funny-looking fat guy were just weird decorations and left it at that. As I got older, I realized that this funny-looking fat guy was pretty important to a lot of people. I wasn't sure if he was their god or not, and while I felt an odd connection to him, I got the feeling he wasn't mine, which in turn left me to wonder who was? I concluded that it had to be that other fat guy, the one that wore the red suit and brought us all of those presents every year. That had to be it! Even with that determination, I still liked the half-naked, fat, Chinese dude better … I just didn't know why.

It was around this time that I discovered the television show *Kung Fu*. From the moment I first watched it, I was mesmerized. Completely hooked! The martial arts action, the vivid imagery of the exotic, monastic setting, with its beautiful temples and gardens, candles, and incense. The deep silence and tranquility it all portrayed. I had never identified so strongly with anything before in my life. Even though at the time I knew nothing about Eastern religion, culture, or monastic life, it all resonated very deeply within me. There was something intuitively comfortable about it all. Many people report that during their first experience in a zendo or dojo they are overwhelmed with a feeling of "coming home," and this is exactly how I felt whenever I saw a Buddha, and especially when I saw it all come to life on the *Kung Fu* television show.

While I loved the martial arts action on the show, I also felt very connected to the flashback sequences, when the confused, young student, Caine, would seek advice from the great Master Po. Caine would sit before Master Po, looking for answers to his deep, philosophical questions. Master Po would always respond to him with a Koan-like riddle that would always confuse young Caine even more. The exchange would always end with Master Po laughing loudly, and with Grasshopper (Master Po's nickname for young Caine) understanding that the answer to his question was that he was asking the *wrong* question! No matter what, Caine always seemed to be comforted just to be in the master's presence, which made me wish that I too had a place to go, as Caine did; it made me want my very own Master Po! Maybe I had been wrong. Maybe that funny-looking, half-naked, fat guy *was* my god, or at least should have been! Either way I was going to find my Master Po!

I don't know if I asked to go, or my parents saw my interest in the *Kung Fu* television show and took it upon themselves to take me, but one day I found myself walking into a martial arts school. This was no small thing, as in the late Sixties there wasn't such a school on every corner as there is now. While all my friends were playing little league baseball, my mother would cart me several towns away to the tiny, second-floor dojo of a Japanese judo master who barely spoke English.

Walking into that dojo was amazing! It had decorations that reminded me of Caine's monastery, I got to wear a cool, Caine-like outfit, and of course, it had its own Master Po! It was everything that I had wanted it to be—that was until the master started yelling at us louder than I had ever heard anyone yell, and to make it worse, I couldn't understand what he was yelling! After being repeatedly slammed to the mat in an exhausting training session, it became clear if this master had any answers for me he was going to beat them into me!

As I got a bit older and more into martial arts, I became less interested in finding a Master Po and completely into becoming a fighting machine. The first thing to fuel this desire was that I discovered the Saturday afternoon *Kung Fu* movies. Again, I was mesmerized! These movies made the *Kung Fu* television show fights look like they were just dancing around playing patty cake. These guys were incredible! (Actually most of it was ridiculous—great athletes doing gymnastics and showy, useless martial arts with a lot of special effects mixed in, but I was only 10 years old, so cut me some slack!) To a kid these guys were like supernatural, comic-book heroes come to life, and I wanted to be just like them!

That is until I saw Bruce Lee...

Bruce was the man! Bruce made the dudes from the Saturday afternoon *Kung Fu* movies look ridiculous! While they were done up in their kabuki-like makeup and dressed in their kimono-like silk pajamas, doing gymnastic, dance routines that masqueraded as fights, Bruce burst on the scene sporting a rugged, shredded-to-the-bone physique and, at that point, was doing the most realistic fight scenes ever shot. He not only made you believe you were watching real fighting techniques but that with hard work you could learn them as well.

Seeing Bruce Lee was another "coming home" experience for me. It was the catalyst for a deep, intuitive insight that thrust me on a journey away from the fantasy theatrics of the *Kung Fu* movies toward reality-based training, away from delusion in search of martial arts reality.

To his credit, Bruce single-handedly created a martial arts boom overnight. He was light years ahead of his time with his ideas about training. He understood long before everyone else that training in only one style of martial arts was limiting, and that a well-rounded fighter needed to take what worked and add it to their arsenal regardless of what style it came from. He also understood early on the importance of fitness and the role it played in fighting.

The event that was the catalyst for Bruce's departure from traditional training was a challenge fight. As the story goes, when Bruce first came to the United States from Hong Kong and started teaching in the San Francisco area, he infuriated the Chinese martial arts community by teaching non-Chinese students. One opposing teacher was so angry that he challenged Bruce to a fight, and Bruce accepted. This fight turned out to be a pivotal moment in Bruce's martial arts development.

According to eye-witness accounts, the "fight" turned out to be nothing more than a ridiculous dance in which the two took turns chasing each other around the room, finally ending with neither having launched a successful attack, nor having landed a single blow. Bruce attributed this to the fact that they had both relied on trying to apply their traditional, robotic, choreographed training drills to the situation. He realized that unrealistic training had no application in a real-life scenario, and that neither of them had any real experience to draw from.

After this incident Bruce shifted his mindset and training away from the outdated inclusiveness of the traditional "my style is best" view, to an open-minded, inquisitive training that drew techniques from many styles, including Western boxing and European fencing. He realized that training had to be constantly investigated, as what was once thought practical might never have been, and what was deemed practical yesterday might no longer be today.

We see an example of an experience-versus-tradition lesson in one of Bruce's most famous movie scenes. Bruce politely watches a guy break a number of boards. As the guy finishes he turns toward Bruce in an aggressive stance, obviously thinking that he's intimidated our hero. Bruce simply snarls at the guy, "Boards ... don't hit back!" He then proceeds to beat the guy to a pulp.

In an instant we all got it. Bruce took away our awe of the fancy stunts and replaced it with an understanding of reality. Breaking boards didn't give the guy any direct experience of using his skills in a real-life situation; it simply gave him the experience of breaking boards, which, as he painfully found out, had nothing at all to do with fighting.

It was an important lesson—so obvious yet understood by so few. Most students were hung up on the mystical, supernatural aura that surrounded the martial arts at the time. They deluded themselves that they could attain a special ability to perform supernatural types of feats and did not understand that martial arts training involves developing a realistic, practical application of physical abilities through incredibly hard, repetitive work. (I must point out that those perpetuating this mystical aura most were martial arts teachers and Buddhist dharma teachers themselves, but much more on that later.)

Bruce's revelation, and the subsequent training path it set him on, changed martial arts forever. All martial artists owe him a debt of gratitude for his innovative concepts and theories on practical training. That said,

Bruce stayed stuck in those concepts and theories, perfecting them in a controlled environment and never testing them in a real-life situation. He became an expert in the training itself, but not in its realistic application.

Buddhism points to this problem by saying, "Once one's boat reaches the other shore, step onto the land and walk, as there's no longer a need for the boat." Sadly, Bruce stayed on the boat and never stepped onto the other shore. He revolutionized training, but mistook the training, the vehicle, *for* the other shore.

This dilemma is still found in countless dojos and zendos. There are many martial artists that are masters of the training mat and victims of the street, sometimes physically, but always mentally (more on this later), and many meditators that are roshis on the cushion but suffer tremendously in their real lives. Both are masters of their trainings but not of its real-life application. Neither has truly put their mastery to the test. It's a real shame that Bruce didn't, either.

Another incident that piqued my interest during Bruce's time (that's the ancient Sixties and Seventies for you young'uns) involved a martial artist named Joe Lewis. Joe was a big, strong, war veteran who had earned a black belt overseas—mainly by beating everyone to a pulp. He came back to the States and started fighting in karate tournaments (which, at least back then, had no safety equipment and guys really hit each other) and became a sensation on the circuit as he took apart just about everyone he fought. In fact, when he did lose, it was due to the fact that he had to show restraint and follow specific rules, rather than due to the other fighter's ability. Joe knew the difference between a tournament fight and a real fight, and those that did beat him on the mat knew that Joe would hand them their head in the alley.

Joe rocked the martial arts world when he declared in an interview that while he and Bruce Lee were friends and he respected Bruce's train-ing innovations, he wasn't a real fighter, as he had never proven himself and only demonstrated his skills in controlled training conditions with people that suck up to him. And when, in response to Joe's statements, the Bruce fanboys pointed out that competitions were not a gauge of true fighting ability but street fights were (supposedly Bruce had had several street fights in Hong Kong in his teens), Joe responded, "I'm a war veteran that stands six feet tall and weighs over 200 pounds. Bruce is 5'7" and weighs 130…"

Joe never issued a formal challenge to his friend, and Bruce never responded to the statement that he had made about his abilities. It was clear what Joe thought would happen if they did get into a fight in the street, and Bruce did not want to find out.

The martial arts world went crazy! This was martial arts blasphemy! Joe became the most hated man in martial arts, and the martial arts fanboys in typical "protect the master" mode circled their wagons in defense of Bruce, as they justified and rationalized why it was so wrong for Joe to make these statements and right for Bruce to not prove him wrong.

At the time I was stunned. How could someone whose whole career and reputation, even his life, were based on the creation of not only a fighting system but personal fighting abilities not want to prove them? How could his supporters not only accept it but rally around him, supporting his unwillingness to fight, using all the typical martial arts justifications for not doing so? (More on this later.)

Now, before all of you Bruce fanatics put out a hit on me, let me say that I am still a huge Bruce fan! What has changed is that I simply view him and what he did from a different prospective—one that appreciates his great foresight, training methods, athleticism, and, of course, his kick-ass movies, which I still watch over and over, almost 40 years later! Do I wish Bruce would have proven himself? Yes. Do I fault him for not proving himself? No. What I fault him for is that he did not humbly and honestly explain why he didn't.

Since I've been talking so much about real-life fighting, my willingness to let things go without an explanation from Bruce about why he avoided proving his skills in a real-life situation may sound a bit hypocritical, but I also want to discourage you from letting your ego lead you into dangerous situations. As martial artists, each one of us should know that there are plenty of bad dudes who can, and will, kick the living daylights out of us. In fact, our survival depends on our understanding this. That's why nature gave us our fight-or-flight response. It's ridiculous to put ourselves in harm's way on the street or to fight someone we know will destroy us on the mat, simply instead of swallowing our pride and being honest with ourselves and others about our desire to *not* fight.

As much as I want to test my skills in a reality-based scenario, I'm not going to choose to engage a knife-wielding psycho in some dark alley if I can evacuate from the situation or get in the cage with a professional MMA fighter because my ego says to. I wouldn't avoid it, either, because, actually, the best way to improve as a martial artist *is* to lose, and the best way to strengthen our Buddhist practice is to turn toward and face adversity.

Rather than just man up and admit that Bruce didn't want to fight Joe, Gracie Jiu jitsu (who were doing challenge matches at the time that would later become the UFC, but more on this later), or anyone else for that matter, and explain why, Bruce's camp hid behind the age-old excuses that, unfortunately, are still used today. I hear it all the time from martial artists whose training is all about choreographed routines with willing, nonresistant partners. The excuse they proffer the most, and the one I get the biggest laugh from is, "The highest level of martial arts attainment is to never use your martial arts." (I get it. I really do. I have no problem with walking, or running, away from any threat if possible. But *never*?)

These folks then say that the most important reason to train in the martial arts is to develop the spirit and meditative mind, to which I argue,

"Then what the hell is the point of training in a combat art if your priority is not to become skilled in combat? I mean, you can develop your mind and spirit with flower arranging or with the tea ceremony! If you're going to train in the martial arts, then you should do so to develop a realistic proficiency in the skillset it teaches!"

Here lies the real issue. Such people need to justify their *not* fighting, just as Bruce's camp did, because they're *not* training *in* a combat art, or at least not in one that has any reality-based training, or has been proven in any realistic application. I'm sad to say, they either know that it *can't* be applied or live with the constant question of wondering whether it *could* be. Because of their persistent doubts about their training and abilities, they need to keep telling themselves this tired, old excuse rather than face the truth.

There is nothing sadder than a martial artist who lives with the constant question of whether they could really defend themselves or not! Some go their whole lives never answering it. What's worse is, they don't realize that not answering it *is* their answer.

I was in the same boat. I didn't really understand till many years later the valuable martial arts and dharma lessons I had learned from all these experiences. From Caine and the *Kung Fu* television show, to the Saturday afternoon *Kung Fu* movies, to Bruce Lee and Joe Lewis, my journey has ebbed and flowed from traditional martial arts to the modern world of MMA. I evolved to not accept any teaching without experiencing its reality-based application—to not buy someone's talk without seeing their walk.

As the Buddha said about finding truth, "Be a light unto yourself, and don't take their word for it. Have your own experience and find out for yourself." The meditator must see if what is experienced in the controlled environment of a zendo is merely the result of *being* in that controlled environment. Does the experience change when the conditions change?

Likewise, for the martial artist, this means to test one's skills against a resisting opponent in a spontaneous, realistic scenario. Do the techniques work? Can they be adapted? Can *you* adapt them?

As I stand across the mat, staring at my opponent, I know that my real opponent is myself. I've gone through this mental process many times during the course of my many years in the martial arts. Through Buddhist practice, I've come to understand it as liberation from an identification with, and attachment to, the ego; as a freedom from conditioning; as an experience of present-moment, real-time aware-ness tempered with a one-pointed concentration—a moment empty of all fixed ideas that gives rise to an untethered spontaneity.

As I stand firm and stare my opponent down, I focus on keeping the moment empty of what the mind would add to it. I let the stream of thought flow by, without getting swept away. It reminds me of my injuries, of how my left arm was once ripped out of its socket during a fight. I throw a few left jabs in the air, and the direct experience of the quick, crisp punches being thrown shows me that any worry that arose from the thought doesn't hold up to the reality of how the arm is now. The arm feels great, and the memory of the injury fades as quickly as it came.

The mind then reminds me that I am 15 years older, three inches shorter, and 20 pounds lighter than my opponent. This raises a mo-ment of doubt, which I respond to with skillful thought. I bring my attention to the level of my experience and ability, and the doubt dis-appears. Others are intimidated by my opponent's kicking skills, and while I have seen others fall to his powerful kicking attack, what they saw as his strength I see as his weakness.

The fight begins, and within my general field of awareness, my concentration quickly focuses on his right foot being lifted ever so slightly off the mat and quickly being put back down. As soon as his foot goes back down, it rockets right back up, throwing a fast, hard round kick.

Had I missed the initial first movement of his foot, I never would have been prepared for it. I have a plan of action in response to his attack, but I'm not attached to it, as the "don't-know mind" knows that my response needs to be natural, spontaneous, for to attach to a plan for a scenario that might happen leaves no flexibility to respond appropriately to the scenario that does happen.

My initial strategy was to step inside the kick and throw a right punch. But seeing his initial flinch allowed me to get so inside the kick that when it landed against my left arm, its impact was minimized, allowing me to trap his right leg with my left arm and sweep his other leg out from under him, which sent him crashing to the mat.

We go to the mat and begin to grapple. Most would think that this would be an escalation of fighting, but it's actually the time that one needs the most patience, as the more one struggles and fights using strength, the less control one truly has. What's most important in grappling is body positioning, weight distribution, and timing. It's not that one isn't aggressive, but the aggression is a slow, constant, methodical process, a step-by-step, moment-to-moment flow, rather than a one-time, explosive use of force.

A grappler adapts to the constant change of temporary conditions in a fight, just as a Buddhist responds to the flux that is moment-to-moment life. A one-time response of sheer aggression that rises out of a panicked desperation is, for the Buddhist, the moment of attachment, when they are caught in their constructed, fixed idea about the situation rather than in the fluidity of a real-time present moment; for the grappler, it's the moment when they mistakenly give us the opportunity that we've been waiting for and get tapped out.

As my opponent frantically tries to change position, he turns his shoulder away from me just enough that I am able to get behind him and "take his back". As I slip around him, I quickly throw my hooks in. Picture me sitting behind him, with him between my legs, his back against my chest, and each of my legs hooked over his. I bring my right arm up over his right shoulder and across the front of his neck, while at the same time, I bring my left arm up to his left shoulder. I grab my left inner elbow with my right hand and secure the lock, as my left hand goes palm down to the back of his head. As I squeeze, putting opposing pressure backward against his neck and forward from behind his head, he taps out before he's choked out.

The mat is where the martial artist finds their truth. It's where they face all their demons and their fears, doubts, and insecurities are exposed. There's no hiding when you're fighting. There's no delusion. You must look clearly at your true self.

This doesn't mean that all martial artists find their truth; many can't or won't look at the reality of the training they are involved in. It's a delusion to think that wearing body armor, using almost nonexistent contact, performing self-defense routines with a willing, non-resistant "attacker," or dancing around doing kata, a choreographed routine of moves done into the air against an imaginary opponent, are viable training methods that can be applied in the real world.

Many martial artists who train in an unrealistic manner have tried to convince me that if they were faced with a real situation, they would suddenly be able to react completely differently from their training. I never understood how they felt they would be prepared for a reality they had never experienced. But that's the insidiousness of delusion. The deeper your delusion, the easier it is for the delusion to convince you that you are not deluded.

In Buddhism, a similar plight is called the "if only" syndrome. The "if only" syndrome is when someone believes that things would go differently, would be better, "if only" they moved, changed jobs, got in a relationship, got out of a relationship, had more money, had less money, were a better Buddhist, became enlightened, and so forth. This is the Buddhist concept of aversion: not accepting your reality. Like the martial artist, the Buddhist is attached to an idea of how they think things *could* be rather than clearly seeing how they *are*.

The irony with the "if only" syndrome is that even when the Buddhist is able to make their reality conform to how they think it should be, rarely does it live up to their expectations, and even if it does bring some satisfaction, it passes quickly and leaves them with yet a whole new set of "if only's" in response. Reality will never match our idea of it. When we can clearly see and face reality, unconditionally accept what we find, and be satisfied with what we have, there is no need for any "if only's," nor is there any need for the martial artist to say, "If this were real..."

An authentic practice is one that, when put to the test, applies the appropriate application in any given situation, one that is *different* from its original conception. Sometimes this difference is minimal and sometimes vast, but it is always different. Real-life scenarios arise as a result of conditions that are in constant flux, so it's necessary to have a practice with applications that are equally fluid in response.

Martial arts or Buddhist teachings are theoretical until tested in real-life circumstances, where they are either proven or disproven as a result. Clinging to theory without testing it is harmful, as it keeps us stuck, whereas testing an application that fails in its real-life application not only conclusively denies its validity but also creates a new theory for future application.

This applies to Buddhism as well. A practitioner quickly learns that skillful application is not dependent on what one *knows* about Buddhism but how one works with Buddhist principles in daily life by learning how to respond with appropriate skillful actions in real-life situations.

As this is also a book about Buddhist practice, let me continue with some stereotypical, seemingly contradictory, Master Po–like, fortune cookie–type, double speak. While I know I've been ranting about how the common traps of the "if only" and "if this was real" syndromes are not reality, the reality is what else *could* they be *but* reality! Or to put it another way: while caught in these traps they *are* our reality, albeit a harmful reality that we don't recognize we're in.

So how do we know when we mistake our delusion for reality? How do we recognize when we are living based on what we think rather than based on how things really are?

It's actually not hard at all! Every time our *idea* of how we want things to be clashes with how things actually *are*, we make the choice to neither avoid what we see or pursue a different view. Instead, we trust our intrinsic knowledge, investigate ourselves with rigorous, unflinching honesty, clearly see our attachment, and immediately break it.

No worries, right? Okay, so maybe it is frustratingly hard! But what's not hard is finding the opportunity to do so. The opportunity is always there if we choose to look.

> A meditation student completely unnerved from having a horrible day full of problems rushed to the zendo, looking forward to the tranquility of meditation to relieve the day's stress, as well as to sit and grow in his ability to be calm and accepting. When he told the master this, the master laughed. "Sounds like you had a day full of opportunities to practice and grow, and you missed every one of them."

2

Cause No Harm
The Nonviolence of Violence

Where there is only a choice between cowardice and violence,
I would advise violence.

— GANDHI

A warrior chooses pacifism; all others are condemned to it.

— UNKNOWN

For obvious reasons, before we go any farther, we must discuss upfront the Buddhist doctrine of causing no harm to any living being.

I've heard repeatedly from certain fellow dharma practitioners that I am wrong for mixing Buddhist practice with hardcore martial arts training. You should see how angry they get, how loud, harsh, even *violent* their raised voices and body language become toward me when we discuss nonviolence (actually, the discussion always comes down to how wrong I am). They view any kind of hard-core martial arts training as violent in and of itself, and regardless of if it's ever used or not, as being incompatible with either their Buddhist philosophy or meditation practice.

Many Buddhist practitioners believe that only soft martial arts are legitimate meditative practices, whereas the hard-core fighting arts are not. They are fine with soft practices such as tai chi, which is great for meditative movement and physical well-being but useless for self-defense, and aikido, which could be effective but is always trained in a choreographed

29

scenario with a willing partner and stresses never fighting nor testing your skills in real life.

This seems contradictory to me. Buddhists believe that we must maintain a meditative mindset in *all* activity, ranging from how we eat to how we go to the toilet. Yet, according to the argument some Buddhists put forth to me, when it comes to physical activity, only practices that are slow and easy or performed in a slow and easy way are classified as appropriately meditative.

To my mind, this doesn't make sense. When things are slow and easy, where is the challenge? Try having a meditative mind when you're under pressure and your adrenaline is pumping a million miles an hour! Can you be mindful when you're in the middle of a chaotic situation? Can you stay mindful when someone's trying to knock you out, choke you, or rip off your arm?

Don't worry. I am well aware of what it feels like to be sitting on a meditation cushion in a controlled, conducive environment with the mind racing a million miles an hour. For many of us, this feels like a chaotic, extreme reality. Right now, though, I'm talking about martial arts. My argument is that our ability to be mindful is always best tested in a fast-paced, extreme real-life situation rather than in a slow, comfortable, and artificially controlled setting. Without a threat to our mindfulness, how can we test our ability to apply it in response? An old Zen tale points to this reality.

> During a terrible earthquake, as the monks ran around the temple in hysteria, the temple's master walked into the kitchen area and, in the midst of the chaos, calmly drank a large glass of water. Once the quake had ended, the master and his monks gathered.
>
> "Did you see during the earthquake," the master said, "how while you novices lost all control, I was able to remain calm and simply

enjoy a glass of water. This was due to my mastery of meditation from my years on the cushion."

A young monk who had been in the kitchen, stood, bowed, and said, "Venerable master, that was not water; it was a glass of soy sauce."

Another argument I hear with regards to hard martial arts and violence is that hard, reality-based fighting arts do not jive with Buddhism not only because they are deemed non-meditative but because "hard" is viewed *as* "violent"—violence being understood to be exactly the out-of-control, harmful state that Buddhism and meditation aim to eradicate.

In reality, hard martial arts are *not* rooted in anger or in mindless behavior that causes harm. Hard-style practitioners are not full of negative emotions or harmful mind states when training, nor do they need to be in order to apply their skills in a real-life situation. In fact, the application of their skills would suffer if they were. Application of skills in response to a real-life situation of aggression is not an angry, confused action; it is a nonattached response of wise, appropriate, action stemming from clear intention.

I would like to think that Buddhists who are critical of hard styles, and of the opinion that they are violent and should never be used, would step up and take the same action that I would take to stop an aggressive act, as in both a Buddhist as well as a humanistic context, it's simply the right thing to do.

Years ago, when I first began studying with Buddhist teacher, Noah Levine, he was adamant with regard to his position of advocating non-violence, even in the case of self-defense. But now that he has children, I've heard him say that when he now reflects on what he would do if his children's safety were threatened, he cannot see himself doing nothing (more on this view a bit later).

I've also discovered that physicality itself is an issue for people who have a nonphysical nature, as they seem to equate physicality itself as violent, or at least equate it with aggression or a lack of restraint.

It's no wonder that Buddhists have so many different perspectives and can't agree on the subject of nonviolence, as Buddhism *itself* can't even agree on the matter. Some Buddhists take a black-and-white, literal approach and stand firmly resolved that there should never, ever be use of force under any circumstances. Others see a gray area, where wisdom and intention should dictate a subjective, skillful, and appropriate response to each situation. As you might have guessed, the latter is the view I take and will explore in this book.

First, we must look at the definition of violence. The Buddha said that rather than an action being right or wrong, we should investigate the intention behind the action. With this understanding as a guideline, I define violence as any act done with the intention to cause harm, whether it's physical, mental, or emotional, and I define an appropriate use of force as being rooted in *stopping* this harm. Violence rises out of ignorance, delusion, anger, and fear, while an appropriate use of force in response to violence comes from a mind that sees clearly, from understanding and compassion that's rooted in wisdom.

Nonviolence is not the absence of force but the use of force without harmful intent. While many of my critics call my martial arts a practice of violence, nothing could be farther from the truth. Nonviolence does not mean non-action. I train in and teach the use of force as an appropriate response *to* violence, with my intention behind using force being to diffuse and de-escalate violence.

In fact, my Buddhist practice is the foundation of a use-of-force training that I have developed that focuses on minimizing physical altercations through mindful, respectful, compassionate verbal interaction, and non-injurious control tactics. I have trained numerous law enforcement, security, and mental health professionals who have subsequently utilized it with great success, as have I, when I worked as a bodyguard and as the director of crisis response for a hospital emergency room and psychiatric department.

In fact, the precedent in the security and protection fields (which is identical to Buddhist practice) is to treat all subjects with respect and dignity. This is done with a mandate of not only using professional physical tactics (Wise Action) but also appropriate verbal commands, (Wise Speech). Professionals are taught to ask the subject for compliance rather than order it, as well as to use respectful language such as "Please," "Thank you," "Sir," and "Ma'am" when asking.

This is not only prior to the physical response but during it as well. Many times I have said, "Please come with me, sir," as I have locked on a restraining wrist lock, and then said, "Thank you, sir. I appreciate it," as they walk away with me. I've never experienced these situations as violent. On the contrary, I've found them to be calm, restrained, safe, and controlled; helpful rather than harmful to both parties involved. These experiences have repeatedly proven to me that training in a "hard" style is not only conducive to cultivating a realistic application of meditative ability but necessary.

While intention is the main difference between a use-of-force response and a violent act, when we examine the chain of events leading up to a situation, the distinguishing factor that determines intention is its starting point.

The Buddhist teaching of conditionality, as explained by the 12 Links of Dependent Origination, defines the starting point of a harmful course of action as ignorance. I would say that an act of violence *is* ignorance *itself* and the direct result of a chain of events that is completely void of mindfulness. In fact, mindfulness is the *last* thing that happens in a harmful situation (if it happens at all), as the person acting out violently is out of control *during* the act and then "snaps out of it" in a moment of awareness *after* the fact. This usually takes place as the cuffs go on, as they are put in the back of a police car, as the cell door closes, as they are lying in the emergency room, and so forth.

But in an appropriate use of force, awareness is the *first* thing that happens, prompting a wise view with complete control over one's decision -making process, the choices being made, and the actions that rise from those choices. So if ignorance is the start of a harmful chain of events, then wisdom is the start of a helpful chain of events. The reality is that training in a "hard" reality-based style makes someone *less* prone to use force, as having had the experience of a real situation and learning to be mindful during it eliminates the ignorance that would have one enter into it haphazardly.

As I mentioned earlier, many martial arts teachers, usually tai chi, aikido, and other traditional martial arts guys, teach that the highest level of attainment is to never use one's skills. Their rationale is actually comical. They tell their students that they are being taught skills that are deadly, too deadly to ever use, so the highest attainment is to attain these deadly skills, but don't ever dare use them because they are too deadly. Ha!

You already know I disagree, but here's why. I say that the highest level of attainment is to use one's skills with the intention of serving and protecting others. For me, the true definition of violence is to have the means to stop harm and then choose *not* to. To choose *not* to respond, to choose to let someone get victimized, is not only *not* a high level of attainment but actually makes one complicit and contributes *to* the cycle of violence, as stopping the violent act helps the attacker as well as the victim.

How? Well, perhaps the attacker getting the ignorance beaten out of him is a catalyst for him to clearly see his harmful actions and change his life. Relax! That was a joke ... well, kind of.

What if stopping an attack as soon as possible spares the victim from greater pain and suffering than they would have been subject to had the attack progressed farther? Violent offenders are sick and suffering, and delusion is at the root of the harm they are causing. And while understanding this does not condone their actions, it is this understanding that enables us to use our skills with compassion rather than with malice, which *is* the exact difference between violence and the use of force. When you see this clearly, how can you *not* act?

Buddhist practice teaches us to not have fixed ideas, to not get stuck in mental constructs, that it's dangerous to get stuck in what we "think" is right or wrong. Of course we each have our own understanding of right and wrong that we use as our ethical and moral guidelines in choosing the actions we take. But I think we'd all be pretty surprised about how much we all differ on the subject.

Is peace merely the absence of violence? Can we eradicate violence completely, or is this just a lofty, unrealistic ideal? Does such a noble ideal actually cause the very harm it intends to stop by advocating inappropriate actions, or no actions at all? Do we forego helping someone because of an attachment to this ideal? Do we stand by and watch someone get beaten? A child get abducted? A women get assaulted? When we examine our ideals on a personal level, the gray area hits us hard! It's quite alright if you don't agree with my alternative view on this subject. Let's just not fight about it!

3

Are You Fit to Be a Buddha?

It is not good to neglect the body.
To keep the body in good health is a duty, otherwise we shall
not be able to keep our mind strong and clear.
Inward calm cannot be maintained unless physical strength
is constantly replenished.
Your body is precious. It is your vehicle for awakening.
Treat it with care.
Every human being is the author of his health or disease.

— BUDDHA

You can't get much clearer than what the Buddha said about health and the body! Not only is our well-being our responsibility, it is dependent on our physical health. As a martial artist, the importance of the body and its health has always been a huge part of my life, so when I began Buddhist practice and read these quotes they resonated deeply with me.

But while most Buddhists have read one or more of the above quotes, few seem to give the subject the serious consideration the Buddha stressed it deserves. First and foremost, the body and health are the foundation of the Buddha's first insights and teachings.

As the story goes, before becoming the Buddha, our champ was a wealthy, pampered prince named Siddhartha. Cloistered in his spacious palace, his environment controlled for his pleasure, he had only experienced happiness and beauty, as he was always isolated and protected from the painful realities of life and death.

One day he decided to venture out and was stunned to see for the first time a very old man, a sick man, then a corpse. The trauma of this led him to contemplate the impermanence of things and of his own mortality. Clearly seeing the unfulfilling illusion of his privileged life, Siddhartha renounced his crown and self-indulgent life and became a wandering ascetic. In making his decision, he said:

> When ignorant people see someone who is old, they are disgusted and horrified, even though they too will be old someday. I do not want to be like ignorant people.
>
> When ignorant people see someone who is sick, they are disgusted and horrified, even though they too will be sick someday. I do not want to be like ignorant people.
>
> When ignorant people see someone who is dead, they are disgusted and horrified, even though they too will be dead someday. I do not want to be like ignorant people.

As an ascetic, Siddhartha followed all of the practices of the day. For six long years, he practiced severe austerities and self-mortifications, finally almost starving himself to death. He described the results of his failing effort:

> My body reached a state of extreme emaciation. Because of eating so little, my joints became like the jointed stems of bamboo; my backside became like a buffalo's hoof; my backbone like corded beads; my eyes sunk deep in their sockets, looking like the gleam of water seen at the bottom of a very deep well.

Close to death, he was approached by a young peasant girl who begged him to eat. Realizing that neither living a life of self-indulgence nor a life of mortification had brought him the liberation he had sought, he ate, and in eating, finally found the answer he had been so desperately seeking. He clearly saw that a life lived to any extreme would cause suffering, and that liberation was to be found on the path between all extremes called the "middle way."

When the other ascetics found out that he had eaten, they considered him to have given up and shunned him, but the Buddha said:

> The importance of food was not for pleasure, but for the maintenance of the body so that practice could be sustained. We will take food neither for amusement nor intoxication, but only for the endurance for assisting a holy life.

While the Buddha's first insight was that we cannot escape the inevitability of old age, sickness, and death, he also taught that while attachment to the body as a permanent self causes suffering, so will neglecting or treating it in a harmful way. Using the words *maintenance, endurance,* and *assistance*, he taught that our bodies are precious and that we must properly care for them, that our intention must be rooted in giving them proper sustenance to support our practice. He taught how the well-being of our body directly affects our mental and emotional states, as well as how those states influence our actions, and that all the understanding and insight in the world won't do a thing to fortify a weakened physical state.

My personal example is when I'm hungry or tired, or worse … both! These states of physical weakness leave me with little ability to be patient or thwart my temper. It's simple: giving my body the maintenance of food and rest in turn creates the endurance needed to sustain my practice.

In this same vein, a fighter must understand that the best technique in the world won't mean a thing without a superior fitness level to execute it. Many times, the better fighter loses simply because of a lesser level of endurance, which leads to physical failure. There's no way around it: if a fighter fails at their physical maintenance, they will fail to execute an offense, sustain a defensive strategy, or endure an attack. Ultimately, a knockout or tapout is right around the corner.

So how does a fighter realistically prepare to be fit to fight? By fighting!

While strengthening and conditioning cross training–type workouts certainly help, the only way to truly prepare the mind and body to endure the rigorous intensity of a fight is *to* fight, as nothing else creates the stress that pushes a fighter to the limit.

Even if you run till you drop or lift weights till your arms are like rubber, you won't create the exact mindset or physical response needed to combat an opponent pounding you into the mat. Digging deep to lift that one more rep, or to run just one more mile helps, but the only way to learn how to survive and fight out of a chokehold is to survive and fight out of a chokehold! All the fancy exercise in the world won't prepare you for when you have sweat pouring into your eyes, and your chest is heaving for air, as a guy has all his weight pressing down on you as he pulls his arm tight around your neck.

Now imagine how this could affect a personal protection street situation where failure ends up in serious injury or death rather than a win or a loss in the ring or cage. Imagine if the only reason your child was abducted or your spouse raped was because your body failed and you couldn't effectively respond! I know it's an extreme example, but if someone says that they are training to protect themselves and their loved ones, then to truly do so, they need to fully train for such an extreme situation. Hopefully, that situation never comes, but what if it does?

The same applies to Buddhist practice. It amazes me how so many practitioners don't make the connection between their health and their sitting practice. We often hear how people are directed to use their pain as a teacher, to sit with it and engage it. And while these can be valid instructions at certain times for some people, for most they can be harmful, as their pain is not from the newness of the posture and their inexperience with it, but from their lack of exercise, and the many extra pounds they lug around with them that have already had an adverse effect on them *before* they started sitting. The fact is, if you carry around too much weight for too long, your back and knees will trouble you in any situation, not just in meditation.

Another issue that has always surprised me is how people sit for hours breathing in toxic incense smoke yet don't notice this harmful Buddhist contradiction during their mindfulness meditation. And if they do notice, they are too attached to the ritual of burning incense to put their health concerns first.

What good is sitting if it's causing harm to your body? It's said that the reason Bodhidharma began teaching Indian exercises to monks at the Shaolin temple was to remedy how weak and feeble they were getting from meditating so much and neglecting their bodies. Perhaps unhealthy Buddhists mistakenly equate the body and keeping it fit with ego attachment and vanity. But it's not how you look on the outside; it's about what kind of shape you are in on the inside.

Just Get on the Mat Already!

There are only two mistakes that one can make
pursuing the truth:
not going all the way, or not starting.
— BUDDHA

The weakest of all weak things is virtue
that has not been tested in the fire.
— MARK TWAIN

The journey of a thousand miles begins with a single step.
— LAO TZU

An old Zen story tells of a student who wanted to study with Bodhidharma. The student kept vigil outside the monastery, sitting in frigid winds and deep snow, to demonstrate his sincerity and be accepted. After several weeks with no result, he cut off his arm in a last, desperate effort to gain acceptance.

The point of the story is that to study Zen Buddhism, one must have an unwavering dedication and willingness to go to great lengths to practice, and that a great teacher will demand this of you.

At face value I agree with this. What I don't agree with is the appropriation of stories like these by bogus teachers wishing to portray themselves as "true masters" to more easily exploit students. This issue has come increasingly into focus as Buddhism and martial arts and their cultural differences have made their way to the West (much more on this later).

So do we need a teacher, and if so, how do we find one?

It's been said that if you don't have a teacher you shouldn't study Buddhism. That to study Buddhism without a teacher would at the very least be a waste of time and at its worst would cause harm. According to this rationale, studying on our own would be studying our own ideas *about* Buddhism rather than Buddhism *itself*, and that this would lead to an attachment to our own ignorance and delusion rather than to insight. I would add to this that to study Buddhism with an ignorant and deluded teacher is no different, as one is either being taught a wrong understanding or having their wrong understanding validated.

That said, it can still be helpful to begin sitting without a teacher. Notice that I said sitting rather than meditating. I make this distinction because simply meditating is not exclusive to Buddhism, and Buddhist practice is not simply the practice of meditation, but with a teacher's guidance, a merging of the two does become Buddhist meditation.

By "sitting," I mean the simple practice of getting used to the physical mechanics of posture—starting to pause and rest quietly in that experience, free from any ideas of what it should or should not be, whether it's being done correctly or not, and without a Buddhist context to hold it up against.

I know many experienced meditators might say that this is exactly what Buddhist meditation is, particularly Shikantanza—and they'd be pretty much right. But I must stress that what I am describing here refers to a beginner starting the physical activity of sitting, not a meditative practice that leads to insight as a result of being tempered by correct Buddhist understanding.

To study wrong ideas about Buddhism and then meditate based on them creates harmful delusion and a wrong view of reality, but to "just sit" is helpful, as sitting itself *is* reality. And even if that reality is "bad" sitting, "bad" sitting often can be a *good* experience, as it is a *real* experience. Real experience is our most valuable teacher, as to study is to *think* Buddhism, while to sit is to *do* Buddhism.

It's no different in martial arts training. To study our own ideas about martial arts is harmful. And a bad teacher that is either validating our wrong view or teaching us their own wrong view is even worse. But as I described earlier with sitting, to throw some kicks and punches and begin to introduce our body to the basic physical mechanics of martial arts can be helpful. In fact, as noted earlier, we learn more from a fight, and even more from *losing* a fight, than we ever could from studying conceptual ideas or with a teacher with no real-life experience.

I have met many people over the years who have studied martial arts history and its cultural aspects in great detail, accumulating extensive conceptual knowledge of technique, but who have never stepped on the mat. Such people had studied everything they could about the martial arts, could discuss technique application, and answer any question you asked them. They would ask me questions about obscure historical facts, and when I couldn't answer their questions, took it as proof that I was not a good teacher, thereby justifying their decision to stay on the couch and do nothing. Guys like this would walk into my dojo (and probably every other one in town) and, rather than coming in to finally start training after 20 years of procrastination, they would end up wasting my time talking martial arts with me.

While all the people I've met like this have their own individual issues, the common denominator is that all have rationalized that they need to be at a certain point to be ready to start training, and that this point is reached by gaining knowledge. What they don't realize is that all the preparation they are doing *to* start is exactly what keeps them *from* starting.

People rationalize a million different reasons how they would be better served to not start now. ("I want to lose some weight." "I want to improve my cardio." "I want to be more flexible.") They always have a reason not to start, that once accomplished, will make them better off when they *do* start! The problem is that this place to start, the place to "enter training" never seems to come and they never do.

Many people spend a lifetime preparing to start, only to realize that they never did. The only way to *get* experience is to *have* experience. To think that accumulating knowledge will give us some kind of advantage, give us a better starting point, which in turn will give us better, quicker results, is sheer delusion. This delusion will always keep us from starting, as it perpetuates the idea that *more* preparation will get us to an even *better* starting point, with even *better* results! This keeps us caught in an insidious trap of always pursuing that *better* place to start.

An old Zen exchange illustrates this point perfectly.

> A young student asks the master, "Master, where do I enter Zen?"
>
> "Do you hear the bubbling brook?" the master responded.
>
> "Yes," the student answered.
>
> "Then enter there!" the master laughed.

The student is thinking that there is a special time, place, or situation that one needs to find to begin. Perhaps the student was thinking that the master would tell him to do a special meditation or read a particular holy text, but the master's answer snatches it all away by directing the student's attention to the present moment, pointing to the truth that there is only now. Rather than think about it, the student needed to realize that he was already there. That all there is *is* now. And not only is there no *better* time, there is no *other* time. In the story, the master simply asks the student if he hears the brook. He doesn't direct the student to listen in some special way, or to think about it, only to hear it, to be present for the experience of the moment. This is Zen—being present for the experience of the moment rather than attached to our ideas about it.

So if you want to start meditating, forget about having to rearrange your schedule to create more "free time" or reading up on your Buddhism or gaining more flexibility to start your practice. Just sit down and start right now! Put this rag down and start. RIGHT NOW! And then, once you do start sitting, face your life! Begin integrating your practice into how you live. Turn your wisdom into skillful action. Don't get caught in the "serious" meditator's plight of needing to meditate longer, go on retreat, or become enlightened before applying your practice. After all, after you sit, there's nothing more to do except stand up and fight!

This dilemma doesn't only apply to newbies looking to start training in martial arts and Buddhism. I've encountered many martial artists who have been training for many years stop training and have an incredibly difficult time starting again. The reality is that most don't start again.

I warned one friend that the longer he stayed off the mat, the harder it would be to get back on. Even though he knew better, he responded with the same rationale as a beginner—that he wanted to start again but needed to lose a few pounds and improve his fitness level before he did. Well that was *years* ago, and not only has this idea kept him from getting back on the mat, it's kept him from losing any weight at all! In fact, he's actually gained even more weight. The irony is, had he gotten back on the mat when he first told me he wanted to, the following things would have happened: he would not have gained any more weight; he would have lost the weight that he initially put on in a fraction of the time it took him to gain it; he would have improved his fitness to an even higher level; and he would have years of improved martial arts skills under his belt by now!

An old master once said, "Step on the mat once, train for a lifetime!" Meaning that once you start training, even if you only train once, when you quit you'll spend every day you're off the mat having to face (or avoid) the fact that you quit. This in itself is perhaps the greatest lesson one can learn.

5

CRAMPIN' MY STYLE

Absorb what is useful; discard what is not;
add what is uniquely your own.
All fixed set patterns are incapable of adaptability or pliability.
The truth is outside of all fixed patterns.
Learn the principle, abide by the principle,
and dissolve the principle.
In short, enter a mold without being caged in it.
Obey the principle without being bound by it.
Learn, master, and achieve.

— BRUCE LEE

Most of the old martial arts movies I used to watch as a kid had the same story line: Two schools with different styles of martial arts would each boast that their style was better. Throughout the movie, conflict between members of the two dojos would escalate until it all culminated with a final scene of all the members of each school fighting to the death to prove their point.

For added drama, the movie would open with a scene featuring a member of one of the schools committing an unscrupulous act, immediately telegraphing that it was the "bad" school, thereby making the opposing school the "good" one. This was further accentuated by the "bad" school's students always being dressed in black while the "good" school's students were always dressed in white. Naturally, the "good" guys dressed in white always prevailed.

Ironically, in my own martial arts experience, I was to find that these silly stories weren't that far from the truth. Time and time again in my training history, the great master would pontificate about how our style and its techniques were superior to all others, singling out a particular style and explaining how its technique was lacking in comparison to ours, how its adherents were in some way "bad." It was perhaps no coincidence that the style singled out as inferior was always a style that was gaining in popularity with the public, and not only attracting more new students than our style but leading some of our students to jump ship.

It was ridiculous. Kicking styles would claim superiority over hand technique–oriented styles. Then kicking and striking styles would claim their superiority over joint-locking and throwing systems. Joint locking and throwing systems would then fire back at the striking systems and then ground fighting systems would join in rallying against all of them! To make matters worse, boxers mocked the karate choppers and wrestlers laughed at the grapplers. Way back then, other than the occasional street fight, there were no venues for the claims to be tested, as all competitions were style inclusive.

This all changed in the early nineties, when the Gracie family from Brazil, which traditionally staged dojo and street challenge matches to demonstrate what they felt was their superior form of martial arts, decided to modernize their event concept. They added an octagon, commentators, prize money, advertising, and television coverage and called it the Ultimate Fighting Challenge. In its early days, the UFC was nothing like what it is today. There were no weight classes, no rounds, and no gloves. The only two rules were no biting and no gouging the eyes. Other than that everything was legal.

Early on, Gracie jiu jitsu always prevailed, but as we have seen in the sport's evolution over the years, this had more to do with Brazilian jiu jitsu's newness and fighters' inexperience in defending against it than its superiority over other martial arts. As time went on, more fighters added jiu jitsu to their arsenals, and we saw that what once had been the dominant style become one of many efficient combat tools that every fighter uses. We also saw the evolution of skillsets, as wrestlers devoted their time to developing boxing skills, kick boxers learned how to wrestle, jiu jitsu guys learned how to strike, and to top it all off, all of them realized the importance of their fitness levels and their athleticism in relation to fighting, which led to the addition of elite level trainers and strength and conditioning programs.

Where once the UFC mounted matches that pitted style against style, over the years there has been an evolution in training. Fighters trained in only one style have added other styles to their skillset later in their careers, and the current generation of fighters not only train in multiple disciplines but have been doing so since they started training at an early age. The result is a hybrid fighter with a well-rounded skillset comprised of the most efficient tactics found in multiple styles of fighting disciplines.

Now it might appear that I just dissed jiu jitsu, but the larger discussion of martial arts in this book hinges on my being honest, and I would be remiss to tout the positives of jiu jitsu and not address the negatives.

The reality is that when fighters started adding jiu jitsu to their games, the jiu jitsu-oriented fighters started losing their dominance. This is a sport governed by rules, and even though cage fighting and jiu jitsu matches are realistic— in the sense that two people are engaged in combat, unlike the choreographed nonsense that goes on in Mc'Dojo's with nonresistant partners—it's still a combat sport within boundaries, and these boundaries often need to be erased in a real life-and-death, self-defense situation.

I find that I can defeat the people who typically smoke me when we roll jiu jitsu by the rules if I use techniques from my other martial arts training not allowed by those rules, such as small joint and digit manipulation and nerve and pressure point attacks. In my experience, very few jiu jitsu competitors have any experience in defending against weapons such as a knife or gun, or using weapons like a baton offensively against a threat. I am not saying jiu jitsu isn't an effective martial art for self-defense; I am just saying that, like all other martial arts, it has pros and cons, and in certain areas, uses specific techniques of self-defense that are efficient and can be added to our arsenal.

Today's martial artists don't realize how lucky they are! Back in the day the "our style is best" mentality isolated students and limited them to just one aspect of fighting. If you wanted to learn something else, you had to do it on the down low, as if your primary instructor found out you were training somewhere else, you'd be thrown out of the dojo! I had to spend a lot of time and money sneaking around, going to many different instructors, in order to train in the many different aspects of martial arts.

Nowadays, many schools have moved on from the "one style is best" approach and offer an eclectic curriculum. By employing the most realistic, effective techniques from a variety of different styles, they address all the different aspects of fighting and self-defense in one curriculum. Rather than having to go from dojo to dojo and seminar to seminar looking to satisfy their training aspirations, today's students just have to find the one instructor who's already done it for them. No longer hindered by the rigidity and limitations of one particular style, martial artists now have expertise in many different areas of combat. Whereas at one time it was impressive to be a master of one particular art, it is now seen as a liability, as mixed martial arts masters have reached new heights of ability and elevated the threshold of possibility. It is clear that those in the martial arts field who have not kept up have fallen way behind.

Buddhism has taken a similar path. First, let me be clear. I am not a scholar or expert on Buddhism. I am just trying to talk about the different styles and traditions of Buddhism in the same context as I did with differing martial arts style, and am in no way trying to explain each form of Buddhism. I am going to be making very broad, general statements about Buddhist history, so if you are truly interested in the subject, it really requires a thorough dissection by an accredited academic, rather than my superficial glance based on what I've been taught and have learned via my own practice.

Throughout its history, as Buddhism took root in new places, it was altered by both the cultural trappings and religious beliefs that existed before it. When it made its way from India to China, for example, it merged with Taoism and the many folk religions being practiced at the time. When Indian texts were translated, many Taoist terms were used, and people's understanding of these terms as a result of their already ingrained religious ideas led to their subjective interpretation of Buddhism.

For example, while Indian Buddhists thought of the Buddha as a great teacher, Chinese Buddhists made the Buddha a god to worship and pray to. As Chinese Buddhism spread to Japan, it encountered Shintoism, an indigenous animistic religion that worshipped nature and its spirits. Rooted in the Japanese belief that anything in one's life can be the "way," Japanese Buddhism merged martial arts, swordsmanship, archery, calligraphy, painting, flower arrangement, tea making, and many other activities as meditative vehicles.

The other main trade route, the Chama road, saw Buddhism reach Tibet and Southeast Asia. When Buddhism entered Tibet, it incorporated the native indigenous traditions, customs, and rituals in that country, such as guru worship and the belief in gods, spirits, demons, and the supernatural.

When Buddhism first made its way to the West, it was embraced by many people who were hungry for a spiritual practice free from the dogma of their Judeo-Christian indoctrination. Rather than westernizing Buddhism, followers in the West embraced Eastern culture and its trappings to the point of fanaticism, never realizing they had merely become the Eastern version of the same rigid, conservatism they looked to escape from. I'd go as far as saying that, in the beginning stages, most Western Buddhists followed blindly, more led by their infatuation with the exotic, Eastern cultural trappings than any firm conviction of the merits of Buddhist teaching. I often joke that if "Om Mani Padme Hum" had translated to something like "Thou shalt love the lord, thy god" no one would have embraced Buddhism at all!

As the West's understanding of Buddhism evolved, there was a shift away from people immersing themselves in the Eastern culture that accompanied it to merging their understanding of Buddhist teachings with science, psychology, psychiatry, and even the self-help movement. We have seen both worlds both collide, as practitioners struggle with reconciling the Eastern concept of the "nonself" with the Western concept of strengthening the ego and try to practice renunciation in the midst of the epicenter of materialism.

Like Japan, we have seen other activities become meditative vehicles, but rather than being limited to only the "slow" activities that the East has deemed conducive to meditation, the Western influence has allowed the boundary to be pushed farther. Through their own experiences with mindfulness, Western practitioners have found that activities that were once only thought of as "fixes" for adrenalin junkies, or as mere exercise regimens, can provide the setting for an authentic meditative experience and can be utilized as legitimate mindfulness practices. Surfing, rock climbing, parkour, parachuting, skateboarding, cross training, triathlons, marathons, running, swimming—hell, the West has given the world "the Zen of … well, everything!"

I hope to continue pushing the boundary myself, by promoting reality-based fighting. These seemingly "un-Buddhist" activities, when experienced with an understanding of Buddhist teachings, are no different from sitting on a cushion, as sitting on a cushion without understanding Buddhist teaching is well, just sitting on a cushion. Or is it?

The most galvanizing issue to come out of Buddhism's arrival in the West has been isolating the activity of meditation as its own practice, free from any Buddhist context at all. We've seen this occur in prison settings for stress management, workplace settings for productivity improvement, hospital settings for pain management, and in school settings for attention and behavioral issues. This has caused a huge divide between practitioners.

Advocates say that it makes sense because Buddhism came *after* the Buddha's enlightenment experience—an experience, they are quick to point out, that was derived solely from the practice of meditation. They then continue their argument by saying that the same observations and conclusions that the Buddha came to through meditation are just as available for the secular meditator to discover on their own. Opponents say that practice is not just a practice of being mindful of the moment, of being present, or for some sort of therapeutic result, but that the meditator's sole aim is to realize their true nature, purify their karma, and gain merit for a better rebirth in their future life, so that they may ultimately become enlightened, become a Buddha. In the minds of many Buddhists, this is no different from the Christian idea of sin and redemption, of begging forgiveness to make it to the great afterlife called heaven.

While I don't believe in past and future lives or in a permanent vacation (sorry, I mean permanent enlightenment state), my practice falls in the middle of the two. I strongly believe in the benefits of a Buddhist-free, meditation-only practice, and have experienced them myself. What I have found, though, is that these benefits do not address my deeper issues, and the quality of my life as a whole, unless they are infused with Buddhist understanding, particularly Buddhist ethics. While meditation alone can relieve the surface symptoms, understanding the nature of suffering and the role that my conditioned ignorance and attachment plays in it, and how that translates to my conduct, speech, and thought, is the only route to transformation in my experience.

Simply put, an ass can meditate and get meditative benefits, but they will still be an ass! And while meditating might help them see that the symptoms they seek relief from are a result of being an ass, until they don't want to be an ass any longer, their "Buddhist-free" meditation will actually make them a bigger ass!

The bridge between the two for me is my intention to live in a particular way, one that is different from the past, one that helps to unravel old, harmful conditioning and create new helpful conditioning. My experience has been that this is most effectively done by helping ourselves, but more importantly, by helping others. Meditation alone can be thought of as serving the self; when it's infused with Buddhist understanding, it becomes service to others, which is, in turn, the deepest way to serve the self.

So what has all this got to do with style? Well, as in the martial arts, Buddhism too has evolved in the West from an "our style is best" mentality to a cohesive mixture of techniques and ideas from different disciplines that has created a hybrid practitioner with a much broader knowledge and skillset.

Picture this. Rather than a UFC (Ultimate Fighting Championship) cage fight, a BFC (Buddhist Fighting Championship) zendo match in which two practitioners are engaged in heated dharma debate. Much like the early UFC fighters were limited by their styles, the BFC dharma fighters also have only the knowledge of their particular practice to draw on, and at any time they can be bested in debate by another school—not because the knowledge of their opponent is better but simply because they didn't have that knowledge and weren't prepared to defend their view against it.

Based on this example, we can understand how a Buddhist practitioner of the Theravadan school might be unfamiliar with the teaching of emptiness and be bested in debate by a practitioner from the Mahayana school of Buddhism, simply for lacking training in that teaching. The loss doesn't prove that the Theravadan guy is less of an accomplished Buddhist; it just proves that he practices differently.

So, just as all fighters started learning jiu jitsu and all their fighting abilities improved, Buddhist practitioners who learn the teachings of other traditions tend to up their game to a higher level as well. Today we see Buddhists who actually are putting what the Buddha said about "finding out for ourselves" into practice. It has become the norm rather than the exception to find hybrid practitioners sending out *metta*, or loving-kindness; contemplating koans; scanning the body's sensations during insight meditation; repeating mantras; studying sutras, or sacred Buddhist texts; and reading the writings of the Dhamapadha, Dogen, the Dalai Lama, Thich Nhat Hanh, Ram Dass, Pema Chodron, Jack Kornfield, and my favorites, Stephen Bachelor, Noah Levine, Ethan Nichtern, and Josh Korda.

Though I constantly refer to myself as a Buddhist in this text, and do so in my personal life so that I don't have to explain myself at length about my practice in brief conversations with people I meet, I really don't like using that label. Of course, on one level, I am a Buddhist, as I practice what the Buddha taught. But I'm certainly not what you would call a religious practitioner, one who subscribes to the many trappings, rituals, and beliefs added to the Buddha's teachings, after the fact.

The irony is that the most devout Buddhist practitioners have made all the added-on stuff, the beliefs that came from different folk religions and cultural trappings in the different countries that embraced Buddhism, the most revered part of their practice. What's harmful about this is that it makes people new to Buddhism think that if they do not follow suit, they are not practicing seriously, when it's really the exact opposite! In reality, to be the most stringent, orthodox, conservative Buddhist, one would practice *only* the teachings attributed to the Buddha himself, not what was added *after* the fact!

That said, whatever works for you works for you, and whatever works for me works for me. My point is always that each of us must be clear about what really works for us, though my experience has been that practitioners that are of the "our style is best" mentality whether it be in Buddhism or martial arts, rather than benefitting from their one style approach, end up stuck as they are just crampin' their own style.

6

THE GOOD OF BAD TRAINING: FINDING THE RIGHT TEACHER

He who dares teach must never cease to learn.
— UNKNOWN

*The mediocre teacher tells, the good teacher explains,
the superior teacher demonstrates, the great teacher inspires.*
— WILLIAM ARTHUR WARD

I have over 40 years of martial arts training under my belt, and while this probably seems impressive, I can honestly say that much of it wasn't serious. Now most would assume that *I* wasn't serious, but nothing could be farther from the truth. The fact is, I was always nothing *but* serious. It was the training itself that wasn't serious. Or better yet, the training was serious, and my attitude toward the training was serious, but the material being trained could not realistically support my goals. No matter how serious one is about bad training, it's still bad training!

If you are wondering why the hell did I stick with bad training for such a long time? Well, first let me clarify that the bad training I experienced was not a singular experience. It was a long arduous process to find both the training I wanted and the right person to teach it to me.

Over the years my search for the right teachers and the right training has led me to many different teachers in many different disciplines, and while many of my experiences were disappointing, they were absolutely necessary, as seeing what I *wasn't* looking for clarified my vision of what I *was* looking for. And this is important, for what I deem bad training is based solely on my strictly defined goals, and might be exceptional training for someone with different goals in mind.

Which leads us to the real underlying issue: the teacher.

Whether a student is clear about their training goals or has no idea what they are looking for, it is the teacher's responsibility to be able to clearly articulate what a student can expect to learn from them. You would think that this would be easy, but actually, it's then that things get complicated!

Let's look at a few of the difficult scenarios that can arise when a student has specific goals in mind.

The first scenario is that the teacher says that the training supports the student's stated goals, even though he knows it won't. (Yes, he lies!) He tells you anything you want to hear, just to get you to sign your bank account away on the dotted line. He doesn't care when you realize that he has lied, because he has a guarantee of all the cash, so whether you quit or stay doesn't matter to him.

In the second scenario, the teacher also says that the training supports the goals when they won't, but rather than lying about it like the instructor in the first scenario does, he actually believes it! The common example is the instructor who has never been in a real situation, teaches techniques that have never been tested in a real situation, and yet tells the prospective student that the training will support their goal of being able to realistically protect themselves. This instructor is suffering from the "if it was real" scenario I mentioned earlier.

The third scenario is that the teacher knows that his material will not support the student's goals, but rather than lie and say that it does, the teacher convinces the student that they have the wrong goals and then manipulates the student into defining new ones.

I experienced a version of this during a seminar I was teaching at a tae kwon do school. As I was teaching a judo throw, I noticed a group of students at the other end of the mat enthusiastically watching me teach, even though their Korean instructor was staring at me with a look of disgust on his face. After watching me for several minutes, he came over, defiantly crossed his arms, and angrily barked, "Why you waste time with this? I just kick you!"

"Then just kick me," I said, as I turned toward him. "but you had better knock me out," I added, "because if you don't I'm slamming your ass to the mat and choking you out!"

The room got silent.

"Well?" I challenged.

The teacher nervously glanced around the room, put his hands on his hips, and laughed as he said to me in a warning tone, "Ha! You don't want me kick you!"

"But I do," I said, pleading to his back as he walked away.

The thing that amazed me most about this encounter was that, rather than acknowledging that their teacher had not risen to my challenge to prove his assertion, his students accepted his word that kicking (the only goal of his teaching) would always nullify a judo throw. He then spent the rest of the time at the other side of the mat teaching "special" kicking defenses against judo throws to prove to his students that his style was best and discourage them from having the goal to learn judo.

While these negative scenarios happen more often than not, the most common scenario is that the prospective student has not identified *any* goals. An ethical teacher would help the student identify a goal and be honest about whether their program could help them achieve it or not; instead, most teachers just pontificate about how great their dojo is and tell you why you should join. To be fair, some of what unfolds in a scenario like this one is the responsibility of the prospective student. If you don't know what you want from the training, or you choose a dojo just because it's the closest one to your home, or the cheapest, you'll get whatever they have to offer.

And speaking of what they have to offer, all the certificates on their walls and stripes on their belt don't mean a thing. It's what they can do on the mat that matters! I always get a kick out of the guys who advertise that they are a "world famous 10th degree master!" Duh! If they were world famous they wouldn't have to advertise it! I used to have people walk in my dojo and ask me what rank I was, and I would ask them right back, "What rank are you?"

Most would answer, "None. I've never trained before."

And I would laugh and say, "Well, I guess I can teach you something."

I'm not ranking on rank—when truly earned through hard work and perseverance, it's meaningful. But most people don't realize that the standards and requirements for rank differ drastically from school to school (more on this later), and rank has very little to do with choosing a teacher. Many years ago, we used to joke that someone took the "JFK test," meaning that the person left Asia as a lower rank and somewhere over JFK airport they were promoted to 10th degree!

The sad reality is that the teachers that push their high rank as their most prominent selling point have nothing worth buying. But also remember, there are a lot of great practitioners out there that are horrible teachers. Just because someone is great at what they do doesn't make them great at teaching it to someone else. The only real way to make an informed choice is to participate. Experience *what* they have to teach, and *how* they are at teaching it. If they won't let you try a few classes before signing up, then they've got something to hide and you need to get the hell out of there.

Another red flag is someone who wants all the money up front. It seems like a good deal because it gives you your membership at a huge discount, but why would a teacher want to undersell themselves? Well it's either because they don't care if you quit, or they know you will quit. If a teacher doesn't have confidence that their training will retain you as a student over time, why should you? It's also bad business. If too many students are paid up in full, then there's no cash flow. Without cash flow, it's extremely difficult to sustain a business. It becomes a vicious circle of having to get more and more people to pay in full to make up for a lack of constant revenue.

You know a dojo is in trouble if they start hard selling their members who have already paid in full for a shorter term to upgrade to longer-term membership and pay in full again. These longer-term memberships are usually called "black belt programs" and range from three to four years, depending on how long the student has been training. Some schools even offer lifetime memberships. A woman who had recently moved to my area came into my school asking for a lifetime membership for her 10-year-old son. She had saved a huge amount of money this way at his old school and wanted to do the same with me.

I pointed out the obvious. What good was her previous lifetime membership if she was now looking to sign up at my school (not to mention that this was for a 10-year-old who could decide to quit the next day). Her logic was that her son would still occasionally go to his old school as well as mine, and that she would be saving a lot of money.

Needless to say, I knew she'd never get the kid back to his old school, as life would prove too busy for that inconvenience, and while I was confident in my program, I wasn't confident that I could retain any student for a lifetime. Hell, I couldn't even tell you that I'd have a dojo for *my* lifetime, which was almost definitely going to be shorter than her 10-year-old's!

But to be honest, even though I only offered monthly memberships, I considered it. I mean who wouldn't consider thousands of dollars being forced on you. That's right, *forced*. She wouldn't take no for an answer. What a salesman I was talking her out of spending thousands of dollars! In the end she left without signing him up, and I guess that instead of spending two hundred dollars with me, she went down the street to the McDojo, which easily took her pile of cash.

As always, let the buyer beware! Many students have showed up at their dojo for class just days after paying for these expensive types of money-saving programs, only to be shocked to find it closed and their money gone.

I've experienced all these scenarios over the years, and admittedly have fallen for some of them. I hope I can help you avoid them by pointing them out here, but don't get down on yourself if you occasionally fall for them, too, as they helped me, and will help you, clarify exactly what your training goals are and who the right teacher is for you. As I've said, I eventually clarified my own training goal as being how to realistically protect myself, and got there through the trial and error of different "bad" trainings.

These experiences showed me that I would only be able to learn how to protect myself by using training that was reality-based, not by "performing" a choreographed routine of techniques "against" a willing, non resistant "attacker" who knew the routine and how to "perform" for me in response. I know this sounds ridiculous, but it really is how 99 percent of instructors teach.

It still baffles me how the general public is wowed by demonstrations in which the "attacker" throws a single punch, stops, then stands frozen as the "great master" does a bazillion speed-of-light techniques against him. Or how they don't acknowledge that when the "attacker" runs at the "great master" from, say, 20 feet away, and at the last second the "great master" steps aside and with the flick of a finger flips the guy, that the "attacker" merely ran and did a diving roll; the "great master" had nothing to do with it!

Once, I was attending a wedding and a guy who had heard from another guest that I taught martial arts approached me. "Hey I heard you have a school," he excitedly said, as he sat down next to me. "I study gung fu."

I instantly cringed, knowing that I was about to enter a hell realm! You see, most guys who say they study kung fu really mean that they dance and do gymnastics in silk pajamas and think it's a fighting art. They want to talk your ear off about how they cultivate their chi energy, get weekly acupuncture treatments, buy their herbs in Chinatown, make their own dim sum, and have a Chinese wife.

But when a white guy pronounces it "gung fu" with a Chinese accent, you know you are in for it. I say "in for it" because conversations with these guys always seem to be long, boring, ridiculous conversations about the most obscure, esoteric, supernatural stuff you ever wished you had never heard. And for the record, I think kung fu, chi, acupuncture, and herbs are great health practices, and I've done them all, I just can't stomach the nonsense that the fanatic practitioners spew.

"Great," I said with a smile, scanning the room for my wife, hoping to be saved.

"I train in New York City with an amazing master," he went on. "He's a tiny, elderly Chinese man, but his chi is so strong that he can knock you down without touching you!"

I swear to God that I'm quoting him! For you doubters, the internet is full of ridiculous videos of little Chinese guys in pajamas "demonstrating" this very claim. Please go check it out and laugh your butt off!

Now, once in a while, I indulge these guys, as it's a great laugh, but I wasn't in the mood this time, so I called him on it. "Really," I said, trying to sound legit in my awe. "I would love to meet him."

"Great!" my new friend exclaimed with a smile.

"… and fight him… ," I interrupted, watching his smile instantly vanish. "… and if he can knock me down without touching me, I will close my dojo, get divorced, sell everything I own, bow down, move in with him, and become his disciple. But if he can't, I'll slap his phony ass around and embarrass him for making such a ridiculous claim."

Needless to say, we were done. Not only did he refuse to give me any information on how to meet the "great master," he wouldn't take my contact information to set the meeting up. I've seen it time and time again: students who cling to their beliefs rather than wanting the validity of those beliefs challenged.

This phenomenon of believing in miraculous feats is seen much more frequently in public with demonstrations of board, brick, and concrete breaking. Most people have seen these types of demonstrations and, due to them, have a warped perception of the martial arts. While an activity like "breaking" can be considered a training to develop focus and concentration when done realistically in the dojo, most of the public demos involve a display of, at worst, out and out fraud, and at best, manipulative tricks.

The first issue is the materials themselves. What the average person doesn't realize is that the "great masters" doing the demonstrations have the concrete and bricks made for them and that they can be made as solid as steel or as weak as balsa wood. And while pine boards are by nature a weaker wood, they are also carefully chosen by how dry and brittle they are and based on having no knots in them. I've known of "masters" that actually put their boards in a hot oven to dry them even more and make breaking them even easier!

Also important is how wide they are cut and which way the grain is going. A wider board is easier to break, as is one with the grain running horizontally rather than vertically. But it's not only the materials at issue; it's the manner in which they are broken. Most of the breaking demonstrations the public finds most spectacular would be a good deal less impressive were it not for the suspension of belief involved and an understanding of how the feat is pulled off for an audience.

Look carefully and you will start to understand. The first red flag is the use of "spacers." Spacers are small strips placed in between the blocks or boards to create space between them. The general public suspends their belief and doesn't realize that each breaking board or block actually hits and breaks the one next to it. That what they are really seeing is that when the master hits the initial board or block, it breaks the next one, which breaks the next one, which breaks the next one, and so forth. The master's strike never penetrates the full stack. Most of the time, it is a downward strike that works with gravity to pull off the feat. It's actually much more impressive for a martial artist to break two solid, real boards or blocks with no spacers than a stack of 10 with spacers.

As I've said, legitimate breaking done in the dojo is a great training in focus and concentration, but let me be clear it has nothing to do with one's ability to realistically protect oneself. And that's my biggest problem with it all. The general public and prospective new student are manipulated not only to believe that it does but that the greater the breaking ability, the greater the fighting ability. In fact these martial artists almost always have absolutely nothing of value to teach when it comes to realistically defending oneself. Remember: not only do boards not hit back but neither will you, if that's all you're doing in your training.

I've experienced this suspension of belief within Buddhist circles as well. One example that springs to mind was a talk given by a nun at a Tibetan center, which I was attending.

Now, before you picture a meditation center in Dharmasala with a sweet, slight, elderly Tibetan grandma sipping butter tea with a warm, welcoming smile on her face, I want you to visualize New Jersey and a 40-something white female, with a shaved head, wearing traditional

Tibetan robes, and speaking with a loud, southern drawl. But I digress…

Throughout her lecture, this Tibetan nun referred to the supernatural abilities attained by her Tibetan teachers, and how these abilities are available to us all with our continued practice. The wide-eyed audience around me hung on every word. They *ooo'd* and *ahh'd*, as she talked about telepathy, levitation, changing the weather with one's willpower, and other miraculous abilities that her masters were capable of and that we can all achieve through practice.

She ended her talk with a reference to her Tibetan master, who she claimed was able to fly. At this point, I raised my hand.

"Have you seen him fly?" I asked respectfully.

She looked annoyed. "These abilities take lifetimes to attain. The masters don't like to show these abilities, as they don't want new practitioners to focus on them and distract their practice."

"But have *YOU* seen him fly?" I pushed, interrupting her as she was about to call on someone else.

"To talk about it further is the distraction they are afraid will occur."

"But *you* brought the "distraction" up," I protested.

Her face went from frustration to a smile, as if she had reminded herself that they had prepared her for guys like me and that she needed to stick to the script. "Practice requires an open mind," she said in a condescendingly, pacifying tone. "Buddhism is not a practice to take bits from each tradition. One must be willing to pick one tradition and be completely devoted to it to understand it. Understanding comes with time."

Translation: You are a visitor here, you are not part of our tradition, and you bring with you your own beliefs. So either be willing to drop those beliefs and embrace ours (drink the Kool-Aid) or shut the hell up, because I don't want anyone here to be influenced by your doubt.

As she started addressing someone else, I raised my voice and spoke over her. "It was a simple yes-or-no question."

She paused, seemed about to lose her composure, pulled herself together, and ignored me. Several "kind" people seated around me offered to share with me how they "came to believe" the supernatural aspects of the practice, but I politely declined to listen and left.

This kind of situation was not new to me. In fact, it was hauntingly familiar, as the manipulation of cultural trappings and customs was, and still is, a common form of aversion in both martial arts and Buddhism by teachers who wish to avoid addressing an issue.

The scam most often used in martial arts is the "hide behind the masters" trick. This is trotted out whenever a student either complains about a problem paying their tuition or the material being taught, or more often, what *isn't* being taught.

In my case, my questions were always about material I wanted to learn but wasn't being taught. I wish I had a stripe on my black belt for each time an instructor responded to my question with, "I'll have to ask the master." And then got back to me with, "The master will let you know." This not only never happened but was used every time you asked a follow-up question as a way of frustrating you and getting you to stop asking questions. It also saved the instructor, as it wasn't *his* fault the master wasn't giving *him* an answer.

If, like me, you were persistent and became a royal pain in the ass, the answer would then become "You are not ready" or "Wait till you're a higher rank," which weren't answers at all but merely different ways of avoiding the question. Of course, if you asked *when* you would *be* ready, or asked the question again once you received that higher rank, the whole conversation would then circle back to "I'll have to ask the master."

It was also drilled into you that it was disrespectful to ask the master himself, and that doing so was an act of betrayal, so that if the rare opportunity arose that you could ask the master yourself, you didn't dare. This usually came after you had worked your way up the black belt hierarchy, which mostly happened from your teaching *his* classes for *free* as a required part of your "training."

And if you did have big enough yin-yangs to ask (which I did), the answer would always be, "I'll teach you when you are ready!" It was the realization that I *was* ready, and he just couldn't admit that he didn't know the material that I was asking him to teach, that prompted me to go to my first seminar outside the organization (more on that later).

When I opened my first school, I wasn't surprised when I was instructed to use this type of aversion tactic to deal with difficult students. But I *was* surprised when the "great master" told me that I should make sure that I only go to strip clubs far away from my school, so my students wouldn't see me there and my image wouldn't suffer. I took great pleasure in responding to that one with my best condescending tone, "I don't go to strip bars, but I guess it works because no one has ever told me that they have seen *you* at one."

I was also told never to eat in front of my students so they would think I was a superior human (I swear this is true), and on a lighter note, I was told I could keep my long hair (it was a long time ago) because Steven Seagal had a pony tail and was so popular, it would be good for business if people associated me with him (I told you it was a long, long time ago!).

This was all comical stuff, which, in the scheme of things, really was pretty laughable; by opening a school I placed myself inside the inner, cultlike circle, where the level of loyalty and subservience that was expected of me was beyond belief. In one instance, for example, when a college-age guy who had trained with the great master from five years old till his late teens killed himself, we were "ordered" not to go to the wake or funeral because he was a traitor for leaving the master to go train with another instructor who had left our organization.

Another time, a friend of mine who also had just opened a school within the organization and was having a hard time, met with the great master to ask if he could postpone some financial obligations to the organization until he got a bit more secure. He was told no, that he must pay now and learn to "suffer" for his own good and the good of the organization. I'll never forget him coming out of the building to meet me with tears in his eyes. It was at that moment that he and I decided to leave the organization.

All I really ever wanted was to study and teach martial arts and, hopefully, make a living from it. I was a trusting, loyal guy, and this was used against me at every turn. I had been with the organization for years, opened my school, and left in a matter of a few months. While I can be fiercely loyal, it's also in my nature to not take any bullshit, so at the end, the more they threw at me, the more belligerent and adversarial I became. Behind the scenes, I was preparing to pull my school out of the organization and rallying others (who were all unhappy) to join me (which they did). In public, I became such a problem that the "great master" even cornered my wife and told her I was the black sheep of the organization and that she needed to help get me in line. I swear it was that ridiculous!

When I first opened my school, it was one of seven that made up the core of the organization. At the time, the great master (who was no longer teaching) told me that, soon, he would have dozens of schools that would all be sending him money as he lay on the beach, retired, in Hawaii. Well, it's now over 20 years later, and he has never opened another new school. In fact, after I left and took most of the organization with me, his organization collapsed and shrank to just one school. Not only did he have to go back to teaching, he had to teach more than he ever had to in his entire career. Karma really is a bitch!

I know that I've used up a lot of ink here bashing teachers, but the reality is that without their inner circle of fanboy students around them to push their agenda and insulate them from criticism, they couldn't accomplish much at all. They might make the Kool-Aid, but it's the groupies who serve it, and like all good groupies, you just might wake up to realize that you've been used. So be careful what you wish for, as sometimes what you wake up to is a real nightmare!

7

GOOD TEACHERS GONE BAD

A man should first direct himself in the way he should go.
Only then should he instruct others.

— BUDDHA

Just as there are many phony teachers out there, with their blindly following flunkies, there are many others, teachers that I call "good teachers gone bad." This starts with a teacher who's the real deal and, in fact, is such a great teacher that the students stop focusing on the teaching and end up worshipping the teacher and jockeying with each other to be his or her favorite student.

There are no supernatural claims made that need debunking, no avoidance of questions—just good work being done and much progress being made. So much so that the students develop an inappropriate reverence for the teacher, which translates into harmful actions.

I once experienced this while attending a day retreat at the Tibet House in New York City. The teacher leading the retreat was the famous author of many popular, best-selling books. I had read his writing and not only enjoyed it but had benefitted greatly from it, so I was pretty psyched for the retreat.

The day began with the teacher, who had been hidden in an adjacent room to create a heightened level of anticipation, making a sudden entrance, causing everyone in the room to suddenly spring to their feet, as if their meditation cushions had been hot-wired and they had just had their asses shocked! I have no problem with showing respect to a teacher, but I do have a problem with teachers demanding respect, or getting it by building it into required ritualistic behavior, rather than by earning it and letting students choose to participate. What bothered me in this instance was the way the students seemed to try to best each other in how fast they got up for his entrance, like it was a race to win. It reminded me of how in the martial arts, students seemed to compete for the master's favor by how loud they screamed "Yes, sir!" or how deep and long they bowed to him.

When the teacher announced the end of the interesting and insightful morning session, as with his entrance, everyone in the group, (except me, of course) immediately jumped up and stood motionless, heads down, eyes averted, palms pressed together at their chests, as he made his way through the maze of statues back into the same room where he had been hiding. Once he was out of sight, and everyone had collectively exhaled and relaxed, I made a beeline for the bathroom, only to be stopped by one of the teacher's attendants at the door.

"You have to wait," he said sharply, stepping in front of me and putting his hand up between us. "The Lama is using the bathroom and requires privacy."

Now, first let me point out that this was not a single-person bathroom but one with a number of cubicles able to accommodate several people. I had been painfully holding it in for quite some time, so I wasn't a happy Buddhist at this point. As I resisted my desire to "escort" the guy out of my way and pleaded my case that I was suffering and needed immediate … um … relief, the great lama exited, and I was able to rush in and do my business just in the nick of time!

Ironically, bathroom-related issues are often used as teachings in Zen.

A monk asked Ummon, "What is Buddha?"
Ummon answered, "A dried shit stick." (A stick was that time period's equivalent to toilet paper. Uh, ouch!)

What this koan points to is that no activity is outside the realm of our practice, that even what we view as the most mundane or even the most repulsive activity is Buddha! That what constitutes mundane and holy are just ideas in our mind, separations and judgments we create. So always remember that wiping your ass is just as noble a practice as bowing to an altar, and that we should hold our dried shit with the same esteem and reverence as our mala beads. (Well, maybe not literally *hold!*)

There's a real problem when a teacher and his followers start deciding what's holy and what's not. And while I'm not saying that the great lama even knew of, let alone condoned, how his attendant behaved toward me over use of the bathroom, he does have a responsibility in it, as it rose out of a climate around him. I don't know if the lama thinks that he's so holy that he can't stand and piss with us mere mortals, but his follower surely did, and that's scary, because it's that kind of "holiness" that becomes rationalization and justification for accepting harmful behavior.

Another "good teacher gone bad" experience I've had was with a Zen teacher. One night in the zendo parking lot, I was approached by two sangha members who asked me if I would like to make a commitment to making an ongoing monthly financial contribution to help cover the teacher's health insurance costs. He had just quit his job and given up his substantial income, as well as his benefits, to devote himself to full-time practice and teaching.

I was outraged! How was this wise and skillful behavior? Give up your income and benefits when you had a family that was dependent on it? Ask me and others to help support you? I just couldn't wrap my head around it. Rather than being wise and skillful, generous and selfless, his choice seemed completely reckless and harmful, greedy, and self-indulgent. I simply couldn't get past the audacity to take such actions and then ask us to help pay for it after the fact, not to mention that he didn't even have the yin-yangs to ask me himself!

I said no to the request and never went back. To me, it just stank of desire run amok. Desire running amok seems to be a common thread, which leads me to yet another of these stories.

One of my favorite Buddhist authors was embarking on a book tour. He was financing the tour himself, driving from event to event, which were set up by himself as well as his readers. He was staying with friends and readers along the way, so he put out a request on his blog for help adding events to his tour schedule, as well as for places to crash afterwards.

I was psyched! Since I had wanted to hear him speak for years, and I knew he rarely made it to the East Coast, and when he did, it was not close to where I lived, I figured I'd set up an event in my town, give him a place to crash, and I'd finally get to hear him speak!

After confirming a date with his "assistant" (more on this later), I quickly got a yoga studio to donate the space, made posters at my expense, got a friend to write articles promoting the event in the local hipster rag and on the local webzine, and did all I could do to push it online via social media.

A few weeks before the event the author emailed me, requesting that I try to add another event on another date, which I misread as a request to change *our* event to this other date. I emailed him about changing the date, and received a frantic email back from him, which, in turn, led me to see my mistake and rectify it.

I then got an email from his "assistant," who said (and I quote): "Please be aware that he can be easily flustered, so it's important not to throw any new wrenches his way. I don't want you to suddenly tell him something that you and I have not discussed. Issues shouldn't be thrown on him. He is the guest and the "talent" offering his time to you and your community so it's important that you deal with all problems yourself."

There was more about throwing a great event so that we can do this again in the future, and so on. But really? The Zen master is easily flustered? Because of a friggin' little email misunderstanding over a date mix-up? And as for suddenly telling him something we didn't discuss, while I did misunderstand his request and mistakenly responded, causing confusion, I was responding to him!

He reached out to me first, so how can you give me shit about not discussing things with you first? As for the line about him being a guest and the "talent" offering his time, you kind of left out the part that he was using these events to sell books and merchandise! Don't throw in my face how he's offering his time like it's charity and there's nothing in it for him!

So at this point, you figure this story is going to end now with me saying, the hell with it and that I cancelled the event, right? Well, wrong! This is all just a lead up to my "when good teachers go bad" story.

The plan was for him to come to my house and then we would go to the venue, so the day of the event I reached out to him first thing in the morning, trying to find out what time he would be arriving, and got no response.

I finally got a phone call from him at 6 p.m., an hour before the start of the signing, telling me he was already at the venue and would just wait there and grab something to eat. He also added, "I paid for an hour of parking, is there anywhere I can park for free?" I knew he was on a tight budget, and I understood the success of the tour was dependent on him saving on his expenses, so I told him I would cover his parking and his dinner. I then told him that since he had his car there and was coming to our place after the event, we would walk over and catch a ride back with him. I thought we were both in agreement.

After the amount of organization involved, I was gratified when the event went great! There was a large turnout, all the author's books sold, along with most of his merchandise. As we walked outside after the event, a light rain began to fall.

"Guess we'll head to our place. Where are you parked?" I asked.

"Oh," he said and paused. "I'm going to go out with a friend, so I'll text you and let you know what's going on later." And with that they walked away.

I was stunned. He didn't even make an offer to give us a ride home before he went out with his friend!

"No worries, dude," I said as they walked away. "We'll walk home in the rain."

Honestly, I live at the Jersey Shore, a block from the beach, and we love to walk the boardwalk and do it all the time. Our motto is a rainy day at the beach is better than a sunny day at work, so a little rain on our mile-long walk home along the ocean was fine. It was his complete lack of consideration that was the problem.

My wife and I, along with a friend who had been at the event, went back to our place and enjoyed some food and conversation as we hung out waiting for him. Then I suddenly realized that two hours had passed and I hadn't heard from him. Annoyed, I simply texted him "What's up?" After waiting another hour, making it three full hours of not hearing from him, I texted him again. "Not cool leaving us hanging like this. We have work in the morning. Shutting my phone off and going to sleep. Just get a hotel room. Sorry it had to go down like this."

What the hell did he think? That we'd happily sit around waiting for him to just show up whenever he wanted? The next morning, I woke up to a text from him that he had sent in response to my last one that said, "Sorry. I lost track of time. You still up?" Really! Did he really think after all this that I'd be like, "Hey, thanks for being completely inconsiderate and disrespectful. Now welcome to my home! Can I get you a late night snack and fluff your pillow for you?"

The huge irony was that during his talk, he summed up living the Buddhist precepts as "Don't be a jerk." I was originally going to let him off the hook (for him and for my own practice) and write how I understand that he's human, that he's just a fellow Buddhist trying his best, that maybe I just caught him on a really bad night, that maybe he was going through something that I didn't know about. However, I changed my mind when he added insult to injury several days later on his blog when, in writing about the success of his book tour, he wrote:

> I may have to work out how I can afford hotels. One of the interesting things I keep finding is that no matter how nice the strangers you stay with are, and how nice their homes, they are still strangers and their homes are still unfamiliar. So there's a certain degree of stress added just accommodating oneself to other people, even when they are perfectly nice people (which everyone was on this trip). On the other hand, if I had to get a hotel every night, there is no way on earth I could ever afford to tour at all, given what I make while touring. So this may take some figuring out!

Holy shit! Really? It was tough for you to accommodate us nice people? Was it too stressful for you to blow us off for three hours and not be able to just show up whenever you wanted in the wee hours of the morning? Jeez, if you really need some time to "figure it out," then it really is time for you to sit down and shut up!

I could go on, but I think you get the point.

Okay, so I just shared a whole lot of negative stuff about a few people. Why did I do that? Because it was my real experience, and I needed to share it? No. Remember, this chapter is called "Good Teachers Gone Bad." It doesn't mean these teachers are or aren't good teachers or good people; it simply means that teachers go bad sometimes, and it's all part of the experience. And I'm not saying that I'm any different! In fact, I fail daily in my practice—probably a hundred times worse than the guys

I just threw under the bus! It's just very important that we all realize that teachers are human beings who will fail, and that we shouldn't put them up on pedestals or give them too much power over us.

That said, I do feel that teachers should at least be held to an ethical standard. Namely, if they are married, they don't sleep with their students; they avoid spreading sexual diseases; they are not an active alcoholic or addict; and they do not misuse organizational funds. These are all things that some prominent teachers have been guilty of doing.

We can learn from both good and bad teachers, or even when it's a good teacher having a bad day! My martial arts journey has not only been about finding a teacher whose training had realistic application and could teach me how to stop someone from handing me my head; it has also been about finding a teacher who demonstrated honesty, credibility, and integrity. My journey in Buddhism has been no different, as rather than caring about the right time to ring a bell or hit a wooden fish during a liturgy service, I wanted to learn an effective method of dealing with life's conflicts in order to become skillful in my responses and helpful in my actions. I wasn't looking for something to believe in, but something to *do*. I wanted a practice that could be effectively applied to experience, as well as a teacher who demonstrated its application in their own life.

It has taken many years of "yes, sir-ing" and bowing to undeserving masters and many pontificating gurus to find what I was looking for; or rather, what I *wasn't* looking for. As noted earlier, many martial arts instructors teach useless material, which actually puts their students in danger rather than making them safer, and many gurus push their followers deeper into ignorance and delusion rather than helping them to wake up from it. I've walked out on many a martial arts master with a gazillion stripes on their belt as well as quite a few Buddhist gurus who had received transmission and had the papers to prove it.

Training and practice at their core are about loss. It's about breaking attachments, letting go of what's not useful, and getting rid of what's in the way, so one can see things exactly as they are. It doesn't matter whether you're a martial artist or a Buddhist, as each path is merely a different way of experiencing truth, and most of the truth I have found was due to my desire to find it, rather than from a teacher having it or being honest about *not* having it. I now know that many teachers either didn't have the answers I sought, or they were afraid to share them for fear of pushing me in a different direction, which for them meant losing a student. The truly great teachers I've found not only have taught me all that they had to teach but have urged me to leave them when they had. Hopefully, my wasted time will save you from wasting yours.

8

TAPPING OUT

When I tap, it means that I have accepted the technique,
learned the lesson, and look to apply what I've learned
in the next experience.

— RYRON GRACIE

Now that I've covered finding the right training and teacher, and have talked about how "good" teachers can go "bad," it's time to examine when that "bad" has become bad enough to make us want to end the teacher-student relationship.

One of the hardest things to do in Buddhist practice is to break attachment. We pursue and then cling to the things that make us feel secure and comfortable, many times in spite of knowing that it is harmful to us. So when you realize that the teacher and training is harmful, how do you accept it? And better yet, how do you leave? I know it seems like an easy question to answer, but the teacher-student relationship is complicated, as is the dynamic of the setting around it. Whether it's in a martial arts or Buddhist context, when facing this situation many things come up.

First and foremost, are you ready to give up your rank and standing and start over as a nobody somewhere else? It's easy to think that you wouldn't care about being a big shot in a place where you don't want to be, but the reality is that we feel pride in our achievements (even if the training was useless, we put in a lot of hard work doing it), so to walk away is tough.

I know this first-hand. I have always sought out new instruction, which consistently has made me the new guy on the mat, a place where no one knew me or my achievements. In addition, after owning my own school for nearly 15 years, I decided to close it, which effectively ended my experience of being the top dog and guaranteed I would never be held in such esteem ever again. While I continue to teach seminars and private lessons, I do this at other people's facilities and, while I'm treated with respect, it's quite a difference to be a guest in someone else's dojo rather than head of my own.

Ultimately, it goes back to our intention. If we are more concerned with getting our ego stroked over what belt is around our waist or where we are in the sangha hierarchy than we are with improving our martial arts abilities or deepening our Buddhist practice, we will never be able to break our attachment. If I was able to repeatedly take off multiple black belts and put on a white belt to train in a different art, you too can change whatever situation you are in. That said, few do. People are so attached to the position they hold or the belt they've earned that even when they realize it's bullshit, they can't give up the ego gratification that comes with it.

One story that illustrates this point for me was when a guy who had reached a brown belt and had been training for years at a nearby school made an appointment with me for a free one-hour private lesson, as he was interested in leaving his school and wanted to see what I had to offer.

When we got on the mat, I asked him to show me some of what he knew. After he showed me the usual traditional stuff that you pretty much learn in your first few months, I asked him what he was taught to do against a knife. Sadly, things hadn't changed much in the arts, as he quoted a page right out of the great master's playbook. "At my school, weapon defenses are only taught to black belts."

I asked him if he had ever seen a class where black belts were being taught weapons. Of course, I already knew the answer was no, but I wanted him to come to the same realization that I had had many years before on his own. He seemed to get uncomfortable and was not receptive to me telling him that his teacher was lying to him not only about teaching the black belts but about knowing the material at all.

I tried to soften the blow by saying that even if what he was told was true, what was logical about his instructor knowing it yet choosing not to teach it? I even added, "It's a good thing no one has pulled a knife on you since you've been training! What would you have done? Tell the attacker to wait till you were a black belt and knew what to do?"

By this time it was obviously a sore point with him, but to his credit, he continued with the lesson. I showed him a number of defenses against knives, guns, and clubs. I explained how my philosophy was that the sooner someone started working on something, the better they would eventually be at it, and that while he had just been exposed to the material, this hour of training had better prepared him for an attack than the years he had been training at the other school.

In the end, he stayed at his school. He did take occasional private lessons with me, but he reasoned he didn't want to throw away everything he had accomplished by leaving. I have experienced this scenario many times over the years. It's a shame. Imagine how good he could have gotten if he had trained regularly with me, yet he chose to care more about wearing a high belt in a system that taught nothing and stay in a school he had wanted to leave.

One of my favorite stories from my own journey is when I, too, was in a similar position, years ago, when I finally got sick of all the exploitation and manipulation by the great masters I had been training with and decided to break away and start going to seminars.

The first seminar I attended outside the organization was with Dan Inosanto, an icon in the martial arts world, both for his role as Bruce Lee's training partner and as a respected instructor in his own right. Dan was not only expert in the Filipino martial arts systems, which encompass a huge variety of empty hand, stick, and knife fighting techniques, but also a consummate student, setting the example of always training and learning. He proved this by putting on a jiu jitsu white belt 30 years *after* he had achieved worldwide fame as a martial arts master! With all the achievements in martial arts he could have been attached to, rather than cling to them, he left them behind and moved forward into a new martial art. His humility was inspiring.

I got a personal demonstration of his humility at that first seminar. When I first met him I bowed deeply, my eyes fixed on the floor, and practically screamed, "Good morning, sir!" This was not a special presentation for him, but rather how I had been trained to act.

I was shocked when he laughed, put his arm around me, and said with a smile, "Hi. I'm Dan."

As we posed for a picture, I thought about how the "masters" I had just left demanded that you bow to them regardless of whether they had earned that type of respect or not. Now here was one of the most famous, accomplished martial artists on the planet, with his arm around me. While he was much more deserving of that kind of treatment than my old teachers, he couldn't have cared less about getting it. What I've discovered since is that all the best teachers could not care less, either.

Our greatest fights lead to our greatest victories. While none of us wishes for conflict, inevitably, it is challenge that forces us to dig deep inside ourselves and find our best. So if you're struggling with whether to leave a teacher, remember: You learn more from tapping out than you ever could by staying stuck in their hold, as the longer you stay stuck in a lock and refuse to tap out, the more you'll get hurt.

9

Stop Blaming the Teacher, Already!

Your work is to discover your work and then
with all your heart give yourself to it.
By your own efforts wake yourself; you are the master.
We ourselves must walk the path.

— BUDDHA

Once you've found the right training, and the right teacher to teach it, the reality is that what you get out of the training is completely up to you. I know, I know. I just spent a hell of a lot of ink going on about how training hinged on finding the right teacher. Well, blah, blah, blah! Move on. It's time to stop blaming the teacher and take full responsibility for your training.

Is this contradictory? Of course! Zen is nothing if not contradictory. You must be able to see both sides. See the sameness *and* the difference, and also see the sameness *in* the difference, and the difference *in* the sameness. I know, a bit too Master Po, fortune cookie cliché for me, too, but that don't mean it ain't true.

Let me put it a different way. The teacher-student relationship and the results (or lack thereof) are dependent on both who the teacher and the student are as individuals and how they interact. And to twist your brain a bit tighter, defining ourselves as individuals is completely dependent on the dynamic of the interaction, just as defining the interaction is completely dependent on our actions as an individual. So since we've already looked at the teacher's part in the relationship, now let's take a look at our part in it.

Since I talk so much about real-life situations, many people have the impression that I think the training that goes on in a dojo or zendo is not productive, but this is a misunderstanding. What I *do* think is that training that doesn't take place in the context of a realistic scenario, under realistic circumstances, is unproductive. That is to say, insofar as the material being taught has a realistic application, and training takes place under realistic circumstances to develop that application, then, yes, training is *everything*.

Training is about being proactive, about creating a level of realistic preparedness. The effort that we put into it is just as important as, if not more important than, the techniques themselves. Realistic training is measured by how hard a technique is worked, with "hard" being defined as the effort being utilized. Train with 50 percent of your effort, and you'll be lucky to have any effective technique application at all once the stress of a real-life situation takes over. Put 100 percent into your training effort, though, and you'll probably get 50 percent effectiveness when the adrenaline rush that comes with a real situation kicks in.

No matter how well we simulate realistic conditions, we can never be completely prepared for the spontaneous, unexpected circumstances of reality. As we increase the effort we use in training, we create new aspects to the scenario, which, in turn, creates a new threshold for facing the unexpected and responding appropriately.

An old Zen teaching tells us to practice with urgency, as though "our head is on fire," and that we are mistaken to think that when faced with a real-life situation, we will be able to rise to the occasion with a higher level of response than we have been training at. What really happens is that we fall *back* from the level we've trained at, so we respond based on how we train. We must train with the same urgency with which we wish to respond, and our "head's-on-fire" effort must be consistent.

A Zen master once spoke of how when someone first recites a sutra, it is done with mindfulness and a meaningful internalization, then, as that person recites the sutra thousands and thousands of times, mindfulness is lost and meaning forgotten, as it becomes a going-through-the-motions, empty habit. He said we must recite it each time as if it was the first time, as if it's the only time, the most important time.

This applies to our martial arts training as well. Most of us train almost daily, and it's easy for us to fall into a habit of going through the motions in our efforts. This happens because most martial arts students view their training from the perspective that they probably will never have to face a threat in real life, rather than from the perspective that every time they train, they are training for that one time they *will* have to face a threat. So, each time we train, we must train as though it's the only time, the most important time—like our "head's on fire."

With regard to training, most people in the martial arts world define and measure the effort alluded to in the "head's-on-fire" metaphor as referring to the execution of physical abilities. This understanding is partially true, inasmuch as the use of speed, agility, and strength and the improvement and refinement of these attributes are vitally important; however, these are mechanics that we apply effort *to*—they are the *results* of our effort, not effort itself.

So if we define effort as an applied intensity of energy, where does this energy originate? How do we increase its intensity? The Buddha said: "We are what we think. All that we are arises with our thoughts. With our thoughts we make the world." This statement points to reality in a much deeper way than merely how we apply our effort, but in this context, we can understand it as identifying the mind as the place where effort begins.

Let's look at conscious and unconscious action. An example of unconscious action is breathing, whereas an example of conscious action is deciding to breathe differently. From this simple example, then, we can see that the application of energy that we call "effort" is rooted in mindfulness. As we apply this mindfulness it creates intention, which in turn prompts a choice. This choice is not only to take the actions needed to support the intention but as we act, to bring acute concentration and greater intensity to bear during its execution.

Now let's take the "head's-on-fire" concept farther.

As noted above, most martial arts practitioners only consider this concept as it applies to how they practice in the zendo or train in the dojo, not to real life outside. And if they do apply it in their daily life, many times it's only for the moments that they deem important enough to warrant it or it comes as a frantic, desperate response to a situation after the fact. It was in developing my martial arts attitude of being prepared *all* the time for that *one* time in my life when I might have to fight to save it that led me to see how, before then, I had been picking and choosing my moments to "be" Buddhist, or at least be mindful.

I started to see how I was not prepared to engage all of the moments in my life in a meditative way, which in turn, made my responses less appropriate and skillful the select times I did respond. It helped me see that *each* moment warranted the *same* attention, that *all* the moments of my time were in fact that *one* time.

We must understand that each moment is a "head's-on-fire" moment. That we must always be utilizing our effort, as no matter how mundane or inconsequential it might seem, each moment and what we're doing in that moment is vital. That anything we are doing can be transformative and is an opportunity to create new, helpful conditioning. And most importantly, sometimes the only benefit we're creating is the *habit* of using greater effort rather than *reaching our goal* as a result of making that additional effort.

There have been many, many times in my life when, rather than training or practicing, I would much rather have just chilled on the couch. It was in these moments that I needed to focus my intention and muster a greater effort to keep my commitment. I was always glad I did, as most times, the training or sitting session turned out to be more productive than usual. But even if it turned out to be a lousy night of training or sitting, the consistent benefit was that I showed up, that I trained or sat regardless of the quality, and most importantly, that I improved my ability to apply effort to my training, which in turn strengthened my discipline.

The Buddha said, "It is better to conquer yourself than to win a thousand battles" and "Endurance is one of the most difficult disciplines, but it is to the one who endures that the final victory comes." In a monastic setting, the monk's day is regimented with a planned routine of activity that supports their commitment to a meditative life. It should be no different for us wannabe laymen. We need a daily routine of activity that supports both the discipline of our practice and discipline itself.

One of my favorite Zen stories points out the dangers of an undisciplined life:

A farmer was working when a wandering merchant happened by on the road next to his field, stopped, and called him over. The farmer, needing a break from his exhausting work, walked out of the scorching sun and into the shade where the merchant sat relaxing, leaning against a cart he had been pulling.

"Friend," the merchant said with a smile, "how would you like to be free from doing all this back-breaking labor?"

Before the farmer could answer, the merchant stood up, and in one swift move, pulled a large piece of canvas off the top of the cart, revealing a devil jumping wildly around in a cage. The farmer stumbled backward in terror at the shocking sight. The devil was growling, his fangs dripping with spittle, his bony arms reaching through the bars of the cage as he swiped at the farmer with his jagged claws.

The merchant explained that the devil was only agitated because he had nothing to do, and that if he was given a task, he would not only happily do it but do it in a fraction of the time it would normally take the farmer to do. The merchant then told the devil to finish plowing the field and return to the cage.

As the merchant threw open the cage door, the terrified farmer screamed, but the devil jumped out and ran past him to the field and began working at an incredible pace, finishing the work in minutes as opposed to the hours it would have taken the farmer. The farmer, thrilled with what he saw, excitedly bought the devil. As he handed over every last bit of money he had, the merchant reminded him, "Remember, every day you must tell the devil what to do. Leave no moment unaccounted for."

Over the next few weeks the farmer's life was blissful, as every morning he gave the devil a list of tasks from dawn to dusk which the devil happily carried out without a problem. One day, an old friend visited the farmer, and they went to town and got drunk together. When the farmer awoke the next day, it was late morning. As he groaned from his hangover, he suddenly remembered the devil. He jumped up and ran toward his house. As he approached his field, he screamed in horror, as he saw his house was on fire and the devil had impaled his children on a long pole and was roasting them in the fire.

Now I'm not saying that if we don't have every single moment planned with activity that it will always lead to a horrible result (although most of us can identify with the fact that too much free time can be an unproductive, even dangerous thing). But what I do want to stress is that we ask ourselves if we are using each moment effectively, as well as understand the importance of discipline—specifically, that the *practice* of discipline itself is just as important as the *result* of that discipline. That discipline itself is a result, and that the benefit we get from discipline is this: the ability *to be disciplined*.

I experienced this often when I studied regularly with Noah in New York City. At the time, I was working as an investigator and my days would start at 4 a.m. to go out on surveillance operations, and more often than not, they would last right up until it was time for me to head into New York City from Jersey. This meant that by the time I sat down on a cushion to meditate I'd been up for 15 hours!

I sometimes would ask myself why I bothered, as half the time I was either nodding out during meditation or zoning out during his dharma talk. What I realized was that just *getting* there was more important than what happened when I *got* there, as it strengthened my resolve in practice and created the ability to support that resolve.

And what's amazing is that, many years later, I'm now getting insights from his teachings that I couldn't grasp then. At the time I had considered my practice half-assed at best, but I now look back on it as the most important time of my practice, as it created the foundation that I stand on solidly today.

10

WARRIORSHIP:
THE DISCIPLINE OF DISCIPLINE

If there is any hope for the future, it must surely rest upon the
ability to stare unflinchingly into the heart of darkness.
— AUTHOR UNKNOWN

A master once said, "To be truly awake you must be able to know with which breath you went to sleep and with which breath you woke up." Most of us can't even imagine having such disciplined mindfulness that we could do such a thing; yet, not only is the possibility of doing it always there but it is this possibility that we must have absolute commitment to.

We sit in meditation and are told to follow our breath. When we first receive these directions it sounds like an easy task, but we quickly learn that to follow them is possibly the hardest thing we've ever attempted. To follow the breath is not just to be aware of our breathing but to be aware of every bit of the experience, to experience every little sensation from the most obvious to the most subtle.

At first, most of us don't last more than a breath or two before we are swept off by our thoughts. With time we are able to stay with our breath for longer and longer periods of time and take our awareness to a deeper level, only to find that on any given day we can find ourselves being swept away again by our thoughts, as though we were sitting for the very first time.

Although we are "just sitting," we come to understand that to "just sit" requires effort and diligence, sometimes every last bit we have to offer. So if "just sitting" is such an arduous feat, what does it take to have this same mindfulness every second, of every moment, of every experience in our lives? What does it take to begin our day with our waking breath, be completely mindful of all that we experience in a given day, respond to it skillfully, cause no harm, then end our day with our focus still so acute that we are mindful of the breath we fall asleep with?

This kind of commitment takes an unwavering resolve, a fearless perseverance of unyielding determination, an unwavering tenacity, a spirit so ferocious that not only does it never turn from adversity, it embraces it! A kind of commitment that unconditionally accepts what each moment has to offer. It takes the spirit of a warrior!

An old Zen story speaks of such tenacity:

> There once was a brutal war lord who was so feared that people would flee just hearing of his plans to conquer them. Time after time, this war lord would ride into a village, only to find that all of its inhabitants had fled and it was his for the taking. Once, as he rode into a village, he was shocked to find a lone, old monk standing in the village's empty square. The war lord took this as an insult and angrily drew his sword and yelled, "Monk! Don't you know that you are standing in front of a man that can run you through without the blink of an eye!" The monk stood his ground and without the slightest hesitation said, "Don't you know that you are before a man that can be run through without the blink of an eye!" Hearing this, the warlord sheathed his sword, bowed to the monk, and rode off.

The way of the warrior is the ability to stay fearlessly present, mindful, and concentrated in the moment. To use every bit of resilience to unconditionally accept what's happening, even death. And while we probably will never face being run through with a sword, the dharma practitioner faces the constant threat of being run through by greed, hate, and delusion, and the martial artist faces the constant threat of being "run through" by being victimized in the street. The only way to deal with their respective situations is to realize that they both need to stand as if they *could* be run through without the blink of an eye.

Coming from the martial arts to Buddhism, it was only natural that I identified specifically with the story of the Buddha squaring off with and defeating the devil image of Mara, as well as the concept of warriorship in general, found in the dharma.

Most martial artists have long forgotten the word "martial" and only focus on the word "art." Martial arts as a discipline arose from the battlefield, and more importantly, arose from the need for the persecuted and oppressed to fight back against tyranny. And while now we use the word "victim" rather than "oppressed," and the fight has gone from the battlefield to the streets, the commitment needed to face it remains the same.

Just as the martial artist must train for the reality of a real-life threat, the Buddhist must practice for the real-life fight against the tyranny of their harmful reactive conditioning.

Many students misunderstand the First Noble Truth of Buddhism and think that the Buddha was saying that *all life* is suffering, when what he really was saying is that the *attached, conditioned* life is one of suffering.

My teacher, Noah, says, "Pain is inevitable; suffering is optional." And while I often use the terms warrior, battle, and fight, when speaking about practicing the dharma, and equate the practical execution of the Buddha's teaching to tactics, concepts, and strategies that I've learned through martial arts training, I don't want to suggest that I think life is a constant battle or that practice is a constant fight. On the contrary, the greatest battle or fight is when one *isn't* living as a warrior, when one is living an *unprepared* life, for it's those of us who do not prepare for battle who not only end up in them, but lose them. To be a warrior is to always be prepared to fight, to be proactive, to never let one's guard down; to have a keen awareness and a concentrated mindset at all times; to know that each moment has the possibility of conflict. If the warrior maintains this mindset, he or she can never be ambushed, never taken by surprise. Through living with the understanding and acceptance that at any moment they can face being "run through," the warrior finds equanimity, for to deny or avoid this possibility is to be consumed in fear of it.

While I am using the example of the warrior for how we must face our lives, more importantly it applies to how we face ourselves, as what we overcome within ourselves translates to how we face things outside of ourselves. Our real battle is with our harmful conditioning, facing the constant threat of our attachment to our fixed ideas and our ingrained, habitual behavior.

The enemies of ignorance and delusion are always attacking, using covert operatives like craving and clinging, anger and hatred. To be a warrior is to know that there is always something to do in the fight against this bondage. The enemy of delusion is so deeply embedded that we must be prepared in every second of every moment for its attack. This is why the real fight is when one *doesn't* have the warrior mindset, for to *not* have the warrior mindset *is* delusion.

Delusion's most effective strategy, its most devious tactic, is to have us think that we are *not* deluded. Even worse than not being prepared to fight is to not realize that there is the need to do so. The Buddha said: "He who struggles for truth will have great reward. He who conquers self will be fit to live. He whose mind is free from delusion will stand strong and not fall in the battle of life. Struggle courageously and fight your battles vigorously. Be a soldier of truth, and you will be blessed."

11

There's Nothing Routine About Rituals

I define "spiritual" as any ritual that moves the spirit.
— SHAWN CHRISTIAN ZAPPO

I am not religious, but I like rituals. I like the idea
of connecting an action with remembering.
— JOHN GREEN

Even though it's incredibly important, our ability to be disciplined won't get us very far on its own; we need to apply our discipline to actions that benefit us.

To start with, we need to identify our intentions, then find specific rituals that support them. With our intentions defined and our rituals identified, we then create a routine of practice utilizing them. Before we discuss this, we need to realize that there is nothing routine about a routine or its rituals. First, we need to understand that each of us will have our own unique set of rituals and routine in which we practice them, and second, they will never, ever be practiced the same way twice.

That's right, our routine will never *be* routine! It can't be, as it, like everything else, is dependent on temporary, changing conditions that will constantly challenge us to adapt it. So the most important part of our routine is to not have one, or better put, to have it rooted in change. This allows us to be accepting of how we execute it, as opposed to being frustrated over how we *think* we *should* be executing it.

When we create rigid boundaries that we must stay within, it sets us up to fail, but when we allow ourselves the space to move freely, we can never get stuck. We've all heard the saying, "The hardest part of the journey is the first step," but I disagree. I've seen countless people start martial arts training and dharma study, but have seen few that stick with it. Experts have said that it takes anything from eight weeks to up to six months to create a new habit depending on either how simple or complicated the activity involved is. The harder the activity, the more adversity one faces in participating in it, hence the longer the timeframe to make it routine. Well, I wouldn't call martial arts or dharma study simple, so I'd say you're looking at the six-month plan.

So get it in your head that for at least the next six months you need to keep your commitment, no matter what. No excuses. Sick, injured, or tired—none of it matters. Just do it. Don't worry about how it goes while you're doing it. Just do it. Get your butt on the mat. Get your butt on the cushion.

And this attitude can never change. Long after the habit is created, you'll still be dealing with that part of you that wants to slack off, or worse wants to quit. Stick to the routine, or you'll get stuck in resistance *to* it. Entertain, even for a moment, the thought of "not doing," and you won't. We always lose that argument with ourselves. As long as we give voice to "not doing," we'll listen, as it's the easy way out. And the reality is that at that moment, we really *don't* want to. Routine more than anything, is doing something when you don't want to do it, so if you give yourself the out, odds are you're going to take it. Don't!

My daily routine starts with meditation, but before I go into explaining my routine, this would be the time that all other Buddhist authors would give meditation instructions.

It would go something like this:

Find a nice quiet place in your home where you won't be dis-
turbed. Once you pick this area, adorn it with meaningful Buddhist
items. Pick a regular time. A good time to meditate is in the calm
of early morning or later in the evening. Ask others in the house
to respect what you're doing by being quiet. Wear dark, loose,
comfortable clothing. Turn off your phone and other devices that
might disturb you.

Once seated, pay attention to your posture. It should not be too
loose or too rigid. Your posture should be comfortable and relaxed, yet
enable you to be alert and awake. Bring awareness to the breath. Let
your thoughts come and go. If you find that you've been swept away
into thinking, do not judge yourself over it; just gently remind yourself
to stay present by going back to following your breath...

Well, you know me well enough by now to know what I am going to
say—*To hell with that same old crap!* Every book, magazine, and video
about meditation starts like this, and it drives me crazy! They always address the topic by explaining in great detail about how to create and control your environment, and therefore the experience.

So in keeping with my anti-establishment, reality-based attitude, I'd
like to approach it from a different perspective. What good is it to only
do something in an environment that is conducive to achieving the best
possible results? The real test is to do it under circumstances that are ridiculously *un*conducive to it!

When I first started studying with Noah, it was in a second-floor studio
on the Lower East Side of Manhattan, right across the street from the club
CBGB's. The Bowery was always like a side show, mixed with an erratic
array of people and behavior—drunks, addicts, hipsters, punks... And it
was always noisy as hell! Sirens, horns beeping, people fighting, yelling,
not at all conducive to getting your calm on!

One night, during an entire meditation period, a guy out on the street screamed, "Fuck you, motherfucker" over and over again, which, of course, got the same response right back from other people on the street. What a teaching it became! Who knew you could find equanimity with a mantra like "Fuck you, motherfucker" repeated over and over!

This experience was actually the norm. When it came to Buddhism, it confirmed for me what I had already realized in martial arts: no matter what you can do, you must be able to do it facing the stressful, chaotic, ever-changing circumstances of real life, or it's useless.

Since I've already spoke at length about fighting as an unorthodox meditative practice, and have mentioned things like surfing, skateboarding, and rock climbing as alternatives as well, another meditative challenge that I undertake in my own life is getting tattooed. That's right, getting tattooed is a meditative practice for me.

Now before you scream, "Fuck you, motherfucker" and dismiss me as a completely insane person, hear me out. We always hear the teaching that what makes pain worse—whether it be mental, emotional, or physical—is to avoid it, that the way to accept it is to engage it. Well what better way to test that theory and develop that skillset than to do something painful! Imagine trying to sit in your zendo-orchestrated, new age state of eternal bliss with punk rock music blaring and a needle rippin' up your skin! Could you? Guess what? You could!

Look, I know I'm on the fringe with most of my ideas about meditative practice, and I'm almost off the edge with this one. But to be serious, I've been amazed and downright blissful about being able to maintain a meditative quality of mind during a tattooing session. The reason is that it proves that meditation works! My highly skeptical nature needs to experience that what I do in "normal" meditation can be assimilated into the extremes of real life. It's highly motivating and fuels my return to the cushion time after time, as it strengthens my resolve in traditional practice.

Speaking of traditional practice, let me get back to detailing my daily routine.

I get out of bed in the morning and go right to the cushion. This is not as easy as it sounds. The morning is tough for me. Not because I'm some kind of late-night party animal—well, not anymore—but because of all my injuries.

First of all, I don't sleep very well as pain wakes me up periodically throughout the night, so I'm often exhausted. The inactivity during sleep causes my body to seize up and stiffen overnight, so that getting up is an arduous process of stretching and loosening, just to be able to stand up straight. Many times I'm bent over and shuffling out of the bedroom like a very old man.

Most of the time, the last thing I want to do once I've gone through this getting-up process is to immediately sit down on the ground, especially with my legs crossed. But I stick to my routine and force myself to do it. As I mentioned earlier, there can be nothing routine about our routine, so some days I sit for a half hour, and some days for a mere few minutes, but I do it. My experience has always been that no matter how resistant I am at first, I'm always glad that I did it.

My daily routine starts with meditation, but flexibility in my routine lies not in *whether* I meditate, but in *where* I meditate. At times, my resistance to getting on the cushion is strong, so rather than struggle, I adapt my routine.

I'm lucky enough to live a block from the beach, so when the cushion is not in my sights, the beach is. The fresh air, the sounds of the waves, the warmth of the sun, and the softness of the sand all lend themselves to a great alternative place to sit when I'm just not feeling the cushion. Whether it's the mountains, the woods, or the beach—nature is a great way to experience the oneness and interconnectedness that the teachings speak of.

What's interesting is that I started sitting at the beach as an alternative, only using it as a safety net, so to speak, to make sure I sat; now, though, sitting at the beach has become such a vital part of my practice that, on many days, I do both the cushion and the beach! For the meditation traditionalist who's freaking out about now… CHILL! I also do formal zazen and kihnin (walking meditation) with a sangha, as well as Koan study and dokusan (private interview with a teacher).

Another great lesson that comes from meditating in alternative places like the beach is that attachment to the trappings of meditation can be harmful. As meditators, it's important that we go through a process of examining attachment and contemplating the role it plays in our practice. Without realizing it, many practitioners have a deeply held belief that it's the adornments such as robes, altars, cushions, Buddha statues, and incense that makes their practice authentic, thinking that these things are what legitimizes their practice.

I was no different. At first, sitting at the beach didn't have that same feeling of authenticity for me. After investigating this, I realized that my idea of practice was limited to "special" times, places, and things, and that due to this, I was separating my experiences into holy and mundane, Buddhist and non-Buddhist, meditative and non-meditative.

It was this revelation that pushed me to change what was a limited meditative practice into an expansive meditative life, from having just momentary meditations to living with moment-to-moment mindfulness. And while now it seems idiotic to say that I had to discover "a meditative life," and I still think that it should have been obvious to me, it wasn't. In fact, it was not only a shock but pretty damn depressing to realize how long I had been so unaware of so much of life and how much I let slip due to my lack of attention.

I went through the same thing in martial arts. It was a bleak moment when I realized how long I had been training with little awareness of what

I was really doing, or better yet *not* doing. Why the hell did it take me so long to see that I was involved in useless training with a bad instructor? Most beginners in Buddhist practice end up with many questions. Why did I stay so long in a bad relationship? Why didn't I quit that horrible job years sooner? How did I not say anything for so long? Why did it take me so long to finally do something?

It can take years to answer these questions. This is why it's so important to create a routine of practice and stick with it, no matter what. When we start training or practice, while we are not looking for a fight, we will likely find one, and it's the going-through-the-motions aspect of our routine in spite of everything that keeps us from getting knocked out.

Just as a fighter goes into survival mode based on sheer will and muscle memory, the meditator must create habitual behaviors that take over when the survival instinct kicks in. When an MMA fighter gets hit and stumbles, he's trained his body to react with a takedown attempt. Since he's losing the striking exchange and, in essence, the fight, a takedown of his opponent gets him out of that danger and puts him in a better position to survive.

It's no different for the meditator. When harmful thought hits us, and we are getting knocked out of our wholesome mind state, we need to go into an ingrained survival mode that gets us out of that losing battle and into a better position to survive the fight. Practice is not about aversion, detachment, or indifference. It's about engaging, and yes, sometimes we must grapple with life's battles just as a fighter would. Many times, we must go into survival mode and rely on the sheer will of our commitment and the muscle memory of ingrained helpful, wholesome conditioning created by our discipline with our routine.

While a martial artist doesn't go looking for a fight and the meditator doesn't seek problems out, the only true way to develop our ability to defend ourselves in a personal protection situation, and to be more skillful in how we handle our lives, is through the experience of really doing it. Real situations create real responses. The more routine it is for us to engage, the more comfortable we will become doing it. And the more comfortable we become doing it, the more our responses will be realistically applicable.

It's not easy! Part of our survival mechanism is to avoid pain and seek pleasure, so we need to be careful that our martial arts training or meditative practice do not become practices of aversion rather than engagement, thereby hurting us rather than helping us. Just going through the motions of choreographed techniques against willing partners or reading sutras, chanting, ringing bells, and hitting wooden fishes, without any attempt to realistically apply it in real life, leaves us doing nothing but an empty routine of rituals that leaves us well … empty.

The next part of my routine after I've meditated is to contemplate Buddhist teachings and my aspirations of integrating them into my daily life. In simpler terms, I don't start living my day without reminding myself *how* I want to live it! This sets the tone for my day. It not only creates a mind state that is aware of how I need to act as skillfully as I can but also serves as a touchstone throughout the day for when I'm *not*! It creates a subtle awareness that shows me when I'm not being aware. The teachings and aspirations that I contemplate are an eclectic mix from my Buddhist experience. It's pretty straight-forward, and most of it you will recognize as something you already know and probably practice as well, perhaps with a slightly different spin. For the most part, it's white belt stuff—Buddhism 101, if you will.

Remember, this is *my* way of practicing, and I'm sharing it, not teaching it. Buddha said, "Be a light unto yourself. Don't believe me. Find out for yourself." And I say, "What, *he* said…"

My daily routine starts with acknowledging the Five Remembrances, which gives me reverence and gratitude for another day:

- I will grow old.
- I will grow sick.
- I will die.
- I will lose everything.
- The only thing I can truly call I, me, or mine are the consequences of my conduct, speech, and thought.

Buddhism is often misunderstood as a nihilistic practice, but nothing could be farther from the truth. The Buddhist remembrances I've listed above keep us in touch with our own mortality and the reality of our lives, which, in turn, creates the intention to cherish each moment and live it as authentically as we can.

To take this a bit farther, I further contemplate that there is not even a guarantee of growing old and getting sick before dying! That I must face the possibility that thanks to some crazy accident, the very next moment could be my last! This thought makes each moment even more special for me, and the reality of getting to a ripe old age, getting sick and dying, looks pretty friggin good!

After the Five Remembrances, I state how I intend to live by reciting the Five Aspirations. Many practitioners start their reciting of these aspirations by saying, "May I be…," but I prefer, "I will be…," as I prefer the responsibility of turning these aspirations into skillful action to rest on my shoulders.

"May I…" has just always had that prayer-like vibe for me, like I was asking someone or something outside myself to do it for me, which doesn't resonate with me at all.

- I will be free from suffering and live at ease.
- I will be wise, generous, and loving, rather than stuck in greed, hate, and delusion.

- I will be liberated from my conditioning, from my attachment to fixed ideas, ingrained behaviors, and habitual responses.
- I will be mindful and present, so that my actions are helpful and not harmful.
- All harmful karma ever created by me, due to my beginningless greed, anger, and ignorance, born of my conduct, speech, and thought ... now I reconcile it all.

I feel it's important to point out that I have changed the end of the last line from the traditional version of "... now I atone for it all" to "... now I reconcile it all." The Judeo-Christian mentality of sin and redemption, that we are bad people begging for forgiveness, does not jive with me at all, and atonement is an actual practice of those religions that encompass this belief system.

I prefer to use the word "reconcile," as rather than being a ritual of seeking redemption from something outside myself, based on shame and guilt, I feel it's a practice of understanding, acceptance, and self-empowerment. Atonement is a quicksand-like practice rooted in the suffering of guilt and remorse. It might enable you to keep yourself from being completely swallowed up, but you are always stuck struggling neck deep in it.

Reconciliation is a practice in which your acknowledgment, acceptance, and understanding keep regret from becoming remorse and keep pain from becoming suffering. Atonement keeps us flailing about with our heads just above oblivion, hoping for someone or something to pull us out, while reconciliation is pulling ourselves out, lifting ourselves up!

We do this by making what's called the Bodhisattva Vows, or as I prefer to call them, Commitments. Again because of my staunch anti-religious stance, I've substituted "I commit..." for the traditional version of "I vow ..." that's always used.

- Creations are numberless; I commit to free them.
- Delusions are inexhaustible; I commit to end them.
- Reality is boundless; I commit to perceive it.
- Enlightenment is unattainable; I commit to attain it.

What? How the hell can we free them all when they are numberless? End what is inexhaustible? Perceive what is boundless? Attain what is unattainable?

Whether we can or cannot isn't the point. The point of these commitments is to continually strengthen our own intention and resolve to practice. If you want to save the world, you must first save yourself. These commitments take me from living haphazardly via my harmful conditioning to living steadfastly on a virtuous foundation, which in turn does save the world … from me!

It's not easy, so to begin to actualize these commitments, I start with engaging in the Five Practices of:

- Recognizing I am not separate from all that is.
- I will be satisfied with what I have.
- I will engage all beings with respect and dignity.
- I will realize a mind that sees clearly.
- I will turn suffering into wisdom.

I follow making these commitments with not merely reciting but contemplating the Heart Sutra. The Heart Sutra is probably the most well-known teaching on emptiness. I find it to be imperative to my practice, as to understand emptiness is to understand that nothing has an inherent existence; that everything is temporary, due to its dependence on temporary, constantly changing conditions; that everything we fear is an illusion. It deconstructs our perception, freeing us from the fixed ideas of our beliefs.

THE HEART SUTRA

Clearly seeing the emptiness of all the five conditions, we completely relieve misfortune and pain. Form is no other than emptiness, no other than form.

Form is exactly emptiness, emptiness exactly form. Sensation, conception, discrimination, awareness are likewise like this.

All dharmas are forms of emptiness. Not born, not destroyed. Not stained, not pure. Without loss, without gain.

So in emptiness there is no form, feeling, perception, discrimination, or awareness. No eye, ear, nose, tongue, body, or mind. No color, sound, smell, taste, touch, or phenomenon.

No realm of sight. No realm of consciousness. No ignorance, and no end to ignorance. No old age and death, and no end to old age and death. No suffering; no cause of suffering. No extinguishing, no path, no wisdom, and no gain.

No gain, and thus we live with no hindrance of the mind. No hindrance; therefore, no fear. Far beyond deluded thoughts, this is nirvana.

Followed by a portion of an important koan to me:

THE IDENTITY OF RELATIVE AND ABSOLUTE

Things are not as they seem, nor are they otherwise. To be attached to things is illusion. To encounter the absolute is not yet enlightenment. Each and all the subjective and objective spheres are related, and at the same time, independent. Related, yet working differently, each keeps its own place. Each thing has its own intrinsic value and is related to everything else in function and position.

From the first time I read this, especially the line, "Things are not as they seem, nor are they otherwise," this koan resonated with me. Even before I had a clue about what it meant, I seemed to have an intrinsic knowledge of those first few words and integrating it into my practice has been vital. It speaks to balancing our understanding and experience of absolute and relative truth and not being attached to either; to see clearly that we must attend to the relative truth of the things that arise in the moment, without pursuing or avoiding them; to understand that the ultimate truth is that their existence is dependent on temporary conditions, and there is nothing inherent about them.

One example I love, which illustrates this truth and also fits perfectly with my martial arts slant, is to look at what we conventionally call a fist. When the hand closes, a fist comes into existence. When the hand is opened, the fist no longer exists. The truth of the fist is that it exists only in relation to the conditions involved with closing the hand. "Fist" is a concept of mind, a conventional label used to describe a closed hand; therefore, the "fist" exists in a relative sense, but the absolute truth is that it does not inherently exist.

My slant is that while the fist doesn't inherently exist ("Things are not as they seem"), when a fighter takes that fist and punches an opponent in the face with it, to not block it or duck it ("Nor are they otherwise") will result in their nose being splattered all over their face. The fist might be an illusion, but don't deny the experience of being punched with one!

An old Zen story points to this:

A confused student decides he needs to leave his temple and go on a journey to find the truth. As he's walking out of the gate, he stubs his toe on a rock. As he's hopping around, screaming in pain, he realizes that he doesn't need to go anywhere to find the truth. It has been right there all along. In fact, he has just stubbed his toe on it!

While searching for absolute truth, you'd better watch where you're relatively walking as existence might be empty, but when you bump into it, it sure can hurt like hell! I then move onto the basic foundation teachings of the Buddha, starting with the Four Noble Truths:

- Suffering exists.
- There is a beginning to suffering.
- There is an end to suffering.
- There is a path to the end of suffering.

As I noted earlier, perhaps one of the most misunderstood points of the teachings of Buddhism is the first Noble Truth. When most people first hear it, they think that it is teaching us to accept a life of suffering, but nothing could be farther from the truth! Yes, this teaching points to the fact that suffering exists, but more importantly, it teaches how life itself is made up of temporary experiences that continually come and go, and due to this, there is a pervasive sense of dissatisfaction.

It is this dissatisfaction that fuels our desire to constantly pursue pleasure and avoid pain, which, as the second Noble Truth then teaches, creates our suffering!

The third Noble Truth then teaches us that there is a way to not suffer, and that way is found in breaking our attachment to our desire to pursue pleasure and avoid pain.

The fourth Noble Truth then tells us how we can break that attachment, and that's by practicing the Eightfold Path. Before we explore the Eightfold Path of how to live, let's first look at the teachings that identify for us the three Truths that mark the existence of suffering that we must live with.

The first Truth is pain. We have a body and mind, which causes us pain. We suffer because we avoid the pain, not from the pain itself.

The second Truth is change. Everything is impermanent. We want to be secure in our expectations being met, but we can't be, because they are rooted in ignorance and delusion. We want reality to conform to our idea of it, so we pursue and avoid things to try and make it conform. The more it doesn't conform, the more we pursue and avoid things. We think that this constant pursuit of pleasure and aversion of pain will eventually make things the way we want them to be, but ultimately, all it does is gets us stuck in a never ending circle of suffering. The irony with this is that if we were to face things the way they are, rather than trying to make them the way we want them to be, we wouldn't suffer.

The third Truth is conditionality. Form, feeling, perception, discrimination, and awareness are the conditions that create an experience that we call "self." From this experience we create a construct of self, a fixed idea of a permanent self that is identified with and attached to these conditions. Due to this we continually pursue and avoid these conditions in a desperate attempt to make ourselves comfortable and happy.

But this is a misunderstanding of self and experience. When examined, these conditions are found to be empty, having nothing inherent about them. Emptiness is not a void or nothingness; it simply means that there is nothing permanent, that what we experience is merely based on temporary conditions. We learn to see that we are living via a construct that we've created, rather than in the present moment of experience. We see that what we have been viewing as our experience is really us experiencing what we *add* to it. We experience what we think about it, not how it truly is.

The irony here is that we come to practice in order to transform ourselves, to be liberated. But how can we transform something that we believe to be fixed and permanent? And that's where we get stuck. By being completely identified with and attached to these temporary conditions, we actually make them permanent. The more we try to change this construct of self, the more attached we become to it. And the more attached we are to it, the more the construct becomes the problem, which in turn causes us to attach to it more in the pursuit of changing it!

Ironically, the liberation we are seeking is found not in trying to change the construct of self but to simply let go of our identification with it! This does not mean that we don't deal with the experience that we are facing; it means that we deal *only* with the experience facing us and not add anything extra to it. It doesn't mean we don't exist; we just learn that we exist differently from how we think we do.

So suffering begins when we attach to a fixed idea of a permanent self and its pursuit of pleasure and aversion to pain. Suffering ends when we break this attachment. This is not detachment or indifference, but a state of nonattached awareness, whereby we can be with experience until its natural conclusion without trying to prematurely end it or abnormally prolong it. We learn how to begin to do this by finding a middle way.

12

THE MIDDLE WAY SUCKS, BUT IT AIN'T AS BAD AS THE ENDS

Life is like the harp string.
If it's strung too loose or too tight it won't play.
— BUDDHA

The middle way is to embrace opposites and make
a synthesis of them thus achieving balance.
— TAISEN DESHIMARU

Like karma and nirvana, the Buddhist concept of "the middle way" has found its way into the mainstream vocabulary and like the afore-mentioned terms, has been just as misunderstood and co-opted as well, including in the Buddhist world.

The public (and many Buddhists) have created an image of living the middle way as being a person who is able to sit blissfully or indifferently in an oasis of meditation, oblivious to the world that's collapsing around them. They think the middle way is great because it creates an experience of everything being okay, of feeling good, or worse, of feeling nothing at all.

Wrong! The middle way sucks! That's right, it sucks! Why? Because it's where it all gets real! It's where you make the choice to face things head on, feel every bit of it, relinquish pursuing and avoiding, and just be with it. The correct way to understand "everything being okay" is that we accept things as they are. This acceptance doesn't translate to feeling good or feeling nothing in the midst of it. In fact, it translates to feeling bad … and that's okay!

Stay with me now. If the two opposite extremes of experience are bliss and suffering, then the middle of these extremes is either contentment or pain. If we are practicing the middle way, when we face the trauma, such as a loved one dying, while intellectually we can *know* healthy, helpful things, such as that they're not in pain anymore, or be grateful for having had them in our lives, this knowledge doesn't spare us from the painful grief of losing them. The wellness we experience from practicing the middle way is that while experiencing the grief, we don't turn it into suffering. The irony here is that if we do suffer, it's because we are avoiding the grief, not from the grief itself. As we try not to feel bad, we actually make ourselves feel worse!

This goes for happiness as well. Rather than being satisfied with the way things are, we want them to be the way we want them to be. Rather than resting in the joy that comes from gratitude and appreciation, we find ourselves seeking a greater experience of feeling good, namely bliss. And it's this constant pursuit of the ultimate feel-good experience that leads us into feeling bad. How ridiculous is it that we make ourselves suffer over our good feeling not being good enough! Then to make matters worse, when we do get that ultimate feel-good experience, we ruin it by worrying about it ending!

Take, for example, going on vacation. You book it months in advance. You think about it often as you wait for it to come. Time seems to drag on forever as your desire to go on your great getaway grows. Every time you are faced with a tough time, your mind screams how great everything will be once you're on that vacation! Your boss chews you out … VACATION! Your kids are driving you crazy … VACATION! Someone cuts you off while driving … VACATION! Someone flips you off when you beep at them for cutting you off... VACATION! The dog barks...VACATION! It gets to the point where any and every little thing makes your head feel like it's going to explode if you don't go on that friggin' VACATION ... like yesterday!

So, finally, it's time to go. The stress of anticipation is at its zenith as you run around finishing the packing you swore would be done last week. You're frantically triple-checking that you took care of all the last-minute details. Where are the tickets! Where's the ride! We CAN'T MISS THAT PLANE! Your heart's racing like it's going to explode out of your chest! You're dripping in sweat! You're bickering with your spouse as you impatiently wait to board the plane. After what seems to have been an eternity, you finally board and collapse in your seat, exhausted. The flight is horrible, as your seat TV doesn't work and the guy next to you is coughing and sneezing and the kid behind you is screaming... *Just another hour and I'll be on vacation*, you tell yourself, as you grind your teeth to keep yourself from screaming bloody murder!

You finally land! Why does everyone immediately stand up! You scream in your head! Don't they know they're making it harder to get off the fucking plane! My row is in front of yours ... *MOVE BACK. WAIT YOUR TURN, AND LET ME OFF FIRST!* The energy it's taking to smile at these people as you are secretly planning their bloody murders is killing you! You can barely catch your breath as you impatiently go through the process of getting your bags, finding your way through the airport, and finding the shuttle to your resort. You find the shuttle, make it to the resort, impatiently go through the check-in process, throw your bags in the room, rip off your clothes to reveal the bathing suit you cleverly wore instead of underwear so you wouldn't have to waste a second of time starting your stay in paradise, rush down to the beach, get your lounger, and as you lay back with that first, frosty, cold tropical libation with the little umbrella on top that you've been dreaming of for six long months, you turn to your spouse and say, "I can't believe we have to leave in five days!"

I'd like to think this is an exaggeration, but we all know it's not. How often in our lives do we lose a good thing out of our desire to *not* lose that good thing? The middle way is simply staying where you are with what is and not pursuing or avoiding and making it worse!

But the middle way is not just how we experience an experience. Buddhism outlines eight main experiences that we all have to experience, regardless of our intentions and regardless of our actions. These eight experiences are:

- Pain and pleasure
- Praise and blame
- Gain and loss
- Fame and disrepute

If we are living our life from a place of being attached to our picking and choosing, preference and judgment, at first glance four of these experiences will seem good or healthy and four will seem bad or unhealthy. But when we see the oneness, the sameness, in these experiences, when we understand them as being two sides of the same coin (or possibly have two perspectives on one issue), we see that the experience is not the issue; rather, it is our conditioned relationship to the experience, our habitual behavior in reaction to it.

Understanding this, we see that all experience can be met with the same acceptance, the same equanimity. Now this does not mean we wish for pain or shun pleasure. It simply means that we can be with *all* experience without adding anything to it. When pain is present, we don't avoid it. We don't use aversion tactics like anger and hatred. We simply experience the pain until it's over. When pleasure is present, we don't pursue it by clinging and craving. We simply enjoy it till it's over.

We learn to live like this by following the Buddha's eight-practice path, which is defined as:

- Wise Understanding
- Wise Thought
- Wise Speech
- Wise Action
- Wise Livelihood
- Wise Effort
- Wise Mindfulness
- Wise Concentration

The first two practices of the Eightfold path are wisdom practices and are about our understanding and our thinking. Wise Understanding pertains to our understanding of the dharma, the Four Noble Truths, and the nature of suffering. Wise Thinking pertains to having our thinking rooted in this understanding, which then gives rise to how we intend to conduct ourselves.

The next three practices are conduct practices pertaining to how we speak, act, and make a living. Conduct naturally lends itself to ethics or morals, and is why these practices are often referred to as virtuous practice. But do not think that this is a practice defined by particular moral judgments that all must agree with and adhere to. This is the farthest thing from Buddhist practice. There are as many different conduct paths as there are Buddhists, but I'll get more into that in a bit; for now, we can understand the goal of conduct practice is not to cause harm.

We have to be careful, though, because things we think might be helpful can turn out to be harmful, and things we think are harmful could be helpful. It's important that we are clear about our intentions in order to help clarify things. What helps us tremendously in clarifying our intentions is to make conduct commitments. Some practitioners call them precepts, some call them vows, but I prefer calling them conduct commitments, as for me as it takes the religious morality feel out of it. The five basic commitments that most versions of Buddhism follow are:

- Not to kill
- Not to steal
- Not to misuse speech, be it false, harsh, or idle
- Not to misuse sexuality
- Not to misuse intoxicants

These commitments outline what *not* to do, and are considered renunciation practice. Renunciation practice helps us weaken our unhealthy conditioning. Some teachers say that just the thought of renunciation will do this, but that hasn't been my experience. We can say that we are renouncing something, but if the only reason we are not acting out is simply because the opportunity isn't there, we aren't actually doing anything.

My experience has been that if you want to weaken harmful conditioning, you have to be engaged in it and break attachment to it *during* engagement. Renunciation is not passive; it is an action, albeit a reaction—but an action whereby rather than doing nothing, one must actually do "not doing." The act of "not doing" is what we do to break our attachment to our harmful conditioning and stop the harm we are causing to ourselves and others.

Whether it be creating a wholesome mindset that directs our thinking in a different direction, or physically leaving a situation, whatever we do to not act out is our "not doing." This can be done the moment we have our first unhealthy thought or at first engagement in harmful behavior, or it can take minutes, hours, days, months, or even years to do so. And while it's obvious we will weaken harmful conditioning more the sooner we break attachment to it, any time we break attachment is progress.

Now if it sounds like I'm saying that practice is about screwing up, stopping it, and taking baby steps forward, so that the next time it happens we screw up less and end it sooner, the answer is a resounding YES! But before you say, "The hell with that!" and throw this book out, bear with me. That doom-and-gloom description is true, but it's only part of practice.

Renunciation is a reactive practice that deals with old, deeply ingrained thinking and behavior, so it's important to realize that it takes time and that we are on a path of practice not perfection. We must not be judgmental of ourselves when we do stumble on the path. Many practitioners put themselves under tremendous pressure to keep these commitments perfectly, and when they don't, they punish themselves miserably. But when we act out, rather than punish ourselves for what we view as a failing practice, we need to see what courage and strength it takes to be able to break that attachment and stop in the midst of it! That to persevere and overcome such adversity *is* successful practice.

I liken it to a fighter being choked. When a fighter is caught in a choke, whether they fight it off and escape, or get choked out, no one says that they suck as a fighter, as it's understood that we will all get caught in a choke now and then; it's the nature of the fight. The same goes for getting caught in our old, conditioned thinking and behavior. Don't think that you suck as a Buddhist! We will all get caught now and then, as it's simply the nature of the practice.

Keep in mind that commitment practice should not be a fire-and-brimstone, sin-and-punishment, guilt-ridden, judgmental type of experience. On the contrary: it should be the exact opposite.

The practice of making and keeping these commitments is just that, a practice. It is an ongoing, never-ending learning process that is rooted in understanding, compassion, and forgiveness, particularly of oneself by oneself.

That said, it does not absolve one from taking responsibility for one's actions, nor does it eradicate the consequences. In fact, this practice is completely based on taking full responsibility for one's actions, as well as facing the consequences head on, no matter how painful they might be. It encourages us to dig deeper into the root causes behind our harmful actions and do the hard work needed to dig ourselves out from the layers of conditioning we're trapped under. It's not about success and failure; it's about a slow and steady transformation, supported by loving-kindness for ourselves, free from any self-condemnation.

This is not an easy process to get used to. Early on, when I broke my commitments, it would fill me with horrible self-loathing, which would prompt me to "punish" myself by not allowing myself to practice. If I wanted to meditate, I wouldn't, as I felt that I wasn't worthy and didn't deserve to practice based on how I had "failed." I had this belief that I had to be a "good" Buddhist to have the right to even *be* a Buddhist. The ridiculous irony of this was that the times I needed to practice the most, I wouldn't let myself!

Renunciation is extremely important work that we must be diligent in, and it can be painful and very disheartening, but like I said earlier, it's only part of our practice. The other side of the coin is to create a proactive practice that helps us create new, helpful, healthy conditioning, so that we avoid the situations that trigger that old harmful conditioning and when we are faced with a trigger, we are able to withstand it.

Now "avoid" does not mean "not deal with"; it simply means that if we change our thinking and behavior to being healthy and helpful, we won't find ourselves around the same people and situations that gave rise to those triggers. And when we've done everything right but life throws us face to face with an old trigger, we can handle it differently from the way we used to.

This proactive practice of creating new conditioning has five basic commitments that build from the five from renunciation practice.

- Rather than just not kill, we put our effort into honoring life.
- Rather than just not stealing, we use just what we need and are generous with what we have.
- Rather than just not misusing speech, we use it to be helpful.
- Rather than just not misusing sexuality, we treat all beings with respect and dignity.
- Rather than just not misusing intoxicants, we put our effort into being mindful.

There are two main schools of thought about conduct commitments. Some Buddhists believe them to be black and white and take a very rigid view, with no room for deviation, while other Buddhists believe that how we act is subject to the situation, and that intention behind the action is more important than the action itself.

So with this in mind, let's explore the commitments.

At first glance, all the conduct commitments seem pretty straight forward, but ongoing practice reveals much more to them than meets the eye. Take the first two commitments: Not to kill and not to steal. Right away most say to themselves, *Okay, I didn't put anyone six feet under today, so I got this* or *I didn't rob a bank today so I'm cool*, but when we examine this deeper we see that killing and stealing are much more than just taking a life or robbing a bank. We find that through harmful thought, speech, and conduct we kill and steal time, relationships, friendships, jobs, productivity, emotions, and so on.

This type of subtlety is also found in the rest of the conduct commitments. In regards to misusing speech, most of us don't walk around telling blatant lies or saying hurtful things to people, but do we think about our idle speech? When we speak is there a value to it? Does it serve a purpose, or is it just mindless chatter distracting ourselves and others?

Perhaps the worst misuse of speech is found in what we don't say. How often have we remained silent when something needed to be said, that while it would have been difficult to say, it would have been helpful to ourself or another? Or maybe we haven't lied, but have we left information out or remained silent, knowing that someone would form an assumption that benefitted us, although we knew it wasn't quite reality?

An old instructor of mine did this by hyping himself and his credentials. Prospective students would be very impressed when he told them that he trained the United States marshals. While this was in essence a true statement, everyone made the assumption that the marshals had sought him out and given him a contract as a tactics trainer to train *all* the marshals; in reality, he had merely volunteered his free services every year alongside a number of other trainers who had done the same for a one-day in-service training for a small group of marshals based in one city. I know, because I took part as one of his team. He didn't lie, but what he *didn't* tell people was a misuse of speech that was purposely deceiving.

The last two commitments seem to cause the most discussion and divide among practitioners. The Buddha said that if we had any other energy to deal with as powerful as sexuality, we wouldn't be able to handle both, and no one would be able to become enlightened. Pretty powerful statement! But let's face it, our sexuality can make maniacs out of us at any time, and most of us have had moments we are not proud of in relation to "gettin' some"! But "gettin' some" is really just a small part of this issue. Like not murdering someone is the obvious part of the do not kill commitment, the obvious part of this commitment is if you are in a committed relationship, don't cheat! But after that, it also has its more subtle levels of practice.

There are as many opinions about sexuality as there are Buddhists; really, the act of sex is not the issue. As long as the one, two, or three, or more consenting adults are clear about their intentions, honest with their partner(s), and no harm is being caused, it doesn't matter if it's guy on guy, girl on girl, guy and guy and girl, girl and girl and guy, couple and couple. Go for it!

Now if the previous sentence bothered you in any way, then that's the deeper problem found with misusing sexuality. This commitment isn't about being judgmental and making a moral definition of sexuality for all to follow. In fact it's the exact opposite! It's about treating all beings with respect and dignity, regardless of their lifestyle choices regarding sex, and on a more subtle level treating all people with equal respect without the influence of sexuality.

Treating people differently based on how attractive they are or our attraction to them is a prime example of the subtle harm sexuality can inflict. So whether hot or not, all should be treated with the same respect and dignity. Take a good look at this, and always remember, as studly as you think you are as a "player," when you're dissin' a girl for her lack of hotness, someone else is dissin' you for the same reason!

All kidding aside, the sad reality is that in the hierarchy of hotness, there is always someone above us and someone below us, and the real disrespect is toward ourselves, as we fall all over ourselves to impress someone who's more often than not even interested! Physical attraction's important, but if it's only skin deep, it gets real ugly!

Well, last but not least: intoxication! The Buddha said, "Do not misuse *anything* that intoxicates the mind"—the key words being "misuse" and "anything." When people first start learning about this commitment, their first and only thought is of alcohol and drugs, but there are many other intoxicating things that can be misused and will cloud the mind, and this is why the word "anything" is so important to note.

First let me address all the haters that will say that I am trying to justify and rationalize the use of drugs and alcohol. You're right—I am. Because what this commitment is talking about is the *misuse,* and I am in no way advocating the misuse of alcohol or drugs, just as I am not advocating the misuse of sex, money, food, gambling, and so on. See a point starting here?

Anything and everything can be misused! Even healthy things like training can become harmful when misused.

Right about now, a hater out there reading this is saying aloud, "But drugs and alcohol have an immediate mental and physical effect on the user that can't be avoided or controlled." And to this I would also say, you're right! But I would also say that anything that is misused and clouds the mind does as well. Then the hater would say, "But, under the influence, you can't stop yourself and your mindless, harmful behavior. You must wait till you come down or sober up." Right! Just as someone in the midst of a sex, porn, eating, gambling, or shopping binge must come down in order to get the clarity needed to stop.

If you think I'm playing a game of semantics, I'm not. In my experience, the mental and emotional collapse that fuels and sustains rampant desire and accompanies a binge or addictive experience does not differ due to the exploit of choice.

My own drug of choice is anger. In the midst of an anger binge, I can experience the same immediate loss of faculty and blackout experience described by alcoholics and addicts. I lose control and rational thought, act out harmfully with no ability to stop, and cause consequences without realizing it at the time, and even sometimes not remembering afterward. Many times, the only time I can bring mindfulness and restraint back is after the anger itself has begun to dissipate, just as someone under the influence does as they slowly sober up.

Although those with drug and alcohol problems will take this as me minimizing what they go through, nothing could be farther from the truth. I'm merely saying that other things can be just as caustic when misused, and that there are Buddhists who use alcohol and drugs without harmful effect.

This leads us to the other important part of this commitment that is vital to understand: not to misuse.

Misuse is defined by our intention, by the "why" of what we do and then the subsequent conduct that follows from that intention, or the "how" of it. To get drunk, high, laid, watch porn, gamble, overeat, not eat, shop, even meditate as an aversion-based coping mechanism, or as a way to lash out, would be typical of the harmful intention associated with misuse. It's *why* we are doing it and *how* we are doing it, no matter what the exploit is.

What always baffles me is how many vices other practitioners leave off the list and also the number they fail to see as being an issue in their own lives. For example, during sangha roundtables, I've frequently witnessed practitioners being vocal about this commitment being only about alcohol and drugs, with abstinence the only option, only for them to walk outside afterwards and light a cigarette or consume a huge portion of the most unhealthy thing on the menu at the restaurant, if we then go out to eat.

It's ironic that many practitioners do not realize that many of their favorite Buddhist teachers—people whom they have put on pedestals and whose teachings they quote and reputations they glorify—were drunks, womanizers, sexual predators, and adulterers; yet they criticize the average Buddhist for doing something in their personal lives that causes no harm.

So if you want to come at me, know that I'm just a Buddhist, faithfully married for over 20 years, and I enjoy some wine with my wife at dinner and a few drinks with my friends when we're watching UFC fights. I might not be a Buddhist teacher of great esteem, but I promise you I won't grope you in a private meeting or come on to your wife, so let's drink to that!

If we are truly honest with ourselves, we will see how on so many different, subtle levels we cause harm to ourselves and others! Not only is it shocking when we clearly see this, but it can be overwhelming to think of all the work we have to do about it!

The good news is that on some days, the best we will do is not kill someone or rob a bank, while on others, we will do our very best, with a surprising ability to bring love, kindness, compassion, and joy to every aspect of everything we do. Keeping an awareness of our practice of the commitments, and keeping the commitments themselves on any level, is what's vital, for as long as you don't throw in the towel, you'll always still have a shot in the fight.

So what makes keeping these commitments so difficult? Buddhism identifies five separate experiences and calls them collectively the "hindrances":

- Desire
- Aversion
- Sleepiness
- Restlessness
- Doubt

Now these experiences alone are not inherently harmful; it's our attachment to them that is the issue. When attached to these experiences, each has a harmful behavioral result.

Desire manifests in clinging, craving, and pursuing. Aversion manifests in anger and hatred. Sleepiness is misleading as while it denotes being sleepy or tired, it more accurately addresses laziness, or a lack of energy in doing something wholesome and helpful in support of our practice. Restlessness refers to our inability to calm our mind and points toward fear and worry as the root causes. The last hindrance is doubt. This refers specifically to having doubt about the benefits of Buddhist practice, or having doubt of our ability to do the practice.

For me, calling them hindrances minimizes how detrimental these experiences can be to our practice and our lives if not handled wisely. Drawing from my fighting side, I prefer to call them "threats" and our responses to them "counters." Again, these experiences only become threats due to our attachment to them and the unhealthy actions that follow due to that attachment. In response to them we prevent or break attachment to them by utilizing the following "counter attacks":

- We counter desire by finding satisfaction in the way things are.
- We counter aversion by finding acceptance in the way things are.
- We counter sleepiness with concentration.
- We counter restlessness with mindfulness.
- We counter doubt with patience and trust as we go forward in practice and develop conviction in ourselves and the practice.

The next three practices in the Eightfold Path are meditative, or as I prefer to call them, the mental discipline practices of Wise Effort, Wise Mindfulness, and Wise Concentration.

Earlier, I spoke of effort in the context of the intensity and urgency with which we apply it. Now I will address what we specifically apply it to. Buddhist teachings describe Wise Effort as having four specific applications. The first is to prevent unwholesome mind states like greed, hate, and delusion. The second is to break attachment to them when they rise. The third is to create wholesome mind states like wisdom, generosity, and love. And the fourth is to sustain these wholesome mind states.

Translating these Wise Effort applications to a martial arts context, when faced with a protection situation, the first is applied to prevent negative thoughts, the second is to stop negative thoughts when they arise, the third is to create positive thoughts, and the fourth is to sustain those positive thoughts. To do this requires both mindfulness and concentration.

Mindfulness is a general field of awareness, a sustaining of bare attention. It is the ability to be present with what's in the present, both within us and outside us, without judgment. The purpose of mindfulness is to deconstruct experience to its most conditioned level so that we may experience the three characteristics of existence: the nonself, impermanence, and suffering, in order to see the difference between reality and our idea of reality; that all conditioned experience is ultimately dissatisfying and that there is no permanent self to be found in any conditioned experience.

This does not mean that in order to be mindful, we must think harder; actually it's the exact opposite. When we are being mindful, we let go of the unintentional, random thoughts that the brain continually spews and don't intentionally add anything else, other then gentle reminders of practice, such as reminding ourselves to go back to the breath when we realize we've been swept away in unintentional thinking and are no longer present.

As noted earlier, my big gripe about mindfulness is that according to some practitioners, certain disciplines are valid mindfulness practices while others are not. Tai chi, flower arranging, and archery make the list, for example, but MMA, jiu jitsu, surfing, rock climbing, or taking a shit do not. I mean how could you *not* be extremely mindful of what's happening in your ass, and how fast or slow it's happening, whether it's constipation or explosive diarrhea!

The thing that all their practices have in common are that they are deemed somehow more "spiritual" than other practices, and that they are done painstakingly slowly. My experience has always been that it's much more difficult to be mindful in a fast-paced, chaotic circumstance compared to one that's conducive to it, and that *all* activity, rather than, particular activities are mindful practices. Mindfulness is not about the speed of awareness; it's about awareness of the experience at the speed of that experience.

While mindfulness gives us awareness in the moment, it is concentration that is used to apply an acute focus to an object or activity within that general field of awareness. One great explanation of concentration within mindfulness is to imagine you are at the theater, watching a show. Think of the whole brightly lit stage as mindfulness and the spotlight picking out an actor or detail on stage as concentration: mindfulness gives us a view of the whole show, and we use it to direct our concentration and focus on a particular part of the show. The two mental practices balance each other out, as mindfulness needs concentration to calm and steady it and concentration needs mindfulness to direct and inform it. Working together, these two practices create the opportunity for greater understanding and insight.

And of course, there are a few great Zen stories to further illustrate the importance of these practices.

The first is a story of how the Zen teacher Suzuki always told his students that, "when eating, *just* eat." One day soon after, students were horrified to find him in the kitchen reading the paper at the same time as he was eating. When they confronted him, he just laughed, saying, "When you read the paper and eat, just read the paper and eat."

Humor has always been a poignant way to make a Zen point, as another story shows.

Two monks were walking together when they came to a stream. A beautiful woman stood next to it, obviously trying to figure out a way to cross it without getting her beautiful kimono wet.

"Don't worry, madam," one of the monks quickly said. "I will carry you across."

The second monk watched in disbelief as the first monk carried the woman across the stream and set her down. They then continued their long journey back to their monastery.

After walking for hours in silence, the second monk could no longer contain himself and exploded: "How could you do that? We monks take vows of celibacy! We should never even look at women, let alone touch them or carry one in our arms! How could you?"

The first monk responded: "Brother, are you still carrying her? I put her down hours ago."

My contribution to this genre of Zen storytelling is a story from a vacation that my wife and I went on. All around me were topless women—on the lounger next to me, swimming beside me in the pool, sitting next to me at the pool bar, in line with me for food. For days, I was driving myself crazy, averting my eyes as I told myself not to look, only to find my gaze firmly planted ... well, on their firmness. I felt guilty over my desire to look and angry for my inability not to. Finally, I remembered the Suzuki story, laughed, and said to myself, *When you look at boobs,* just *look at boobs.*

While I'm all for being completely mindful of boobs, perhaps it's best that I start talking about mindfulness practice from a more traditional place. So let's forget about boobs and make a clean breast of things. Sorry, I couldn't resist!

The traditional teachings begin with the four foundations of mindfulness. The first is form. Form is defined as the body's sense doors and their contact with the material world: The eyes, ears, nose, tongue, body and mind. We try and experience the process rather than the content—meaning that we see without looking, hear without listening, smell and taste without savoring or repulsion, touch without discrimination, and have thoughts without thinking.

Simply put, this means that we experience the process without adding anything to it. Within this practice, we anchor ourselves with awareness of the breath, which keeps us from being swept away with the random thoughts the brain constantly thinks. As we do this, we deconstruct the experience to its physical level and experience it as such. We stay present and experience the body's sensations of being as, for example, tight, loose, hot, cold, throbbing, pulsing, without adding anything to it, such as naming the experience as good or bad or attaching a story to it or a judgment.

By not adding anything and just experiencing the physical manifestations, we see the temporary conditions that make up the experience and how they are constantly shifting and changing. We break our identification with the body, which in turn breaks our attachment to the concepts of I, me, or mine. We do this by contemplating the repulsiveness of the body, as no matter what it looks like on the outside, everybody's body is the same on the inside. No matter how hot or not a person is on the outside, we are all made up of the same pus, blood, bile, bone, sinew, tendons, ligaments, waste, and so forth.

We also further contemplate the Buddha's teachings on old age, sickness, and death, accepting our own impermanence and the inevitability of our own demise. When we experience this we are able to break attachment to the body.

The second foundation of mindfulness is feeling. How do we experience our contact with the material world? Is it pleasant, unpleasant, or neutral? What are the temporary conditions that create these experiences? If we understand that our feelings arise from these temporary conditions, we can understand that not only is there no need to pursue or avoid them but that pursuing or avoiding them is what causes us to suffer. The insight that comes from this is that we needn't identify with or define ourselves by how we feel or by our conditioned reactivity, as feelings are not who we are but just passing experiences that we observe as they come and go.

The third foundation of mindfulness is mental states. What state of mind are we in due to our experience of contact and feeling? Is it one of loving-kindness, compassion, or sympathetic joy? Or is it one of greed, hate, or delusion? Is it an experience of equanimity or one of bliss or agitation? Is our mind state wholesome or unwholesome? What are the temporary conditions that create this experience? And again, rather than identify and define ourselves by them, we see them for what they are: temporary experiences based on changing conditions.

The fourth foundation of mindfulness involves all other events and phenomena, including the dharma. Using this practice and our understanding of the dharma, we contemplate the functioning of the mind and the dharma. We contemplate the conditions of the self, namely form, feeling, perception, discrimination, and awareness, as well as the hindrances of the self, namely desire, aversion, restlessness, sleepiness, and doubt, and the experience that has arisen as a result.

Are we experiencing the true, present-moment experience or are we experiencing what we add to it? Are we experiencing past memory or future worry? Are we adding an emotional response exaggerated by a past situation, which pushes us farther away from the present experience, making it impossible to truly deal with what's happening now? Do we see the inter-dependence of all existence, as well as the relation between mind and the material world? Do we see our attachment? Can we see through our delusion? Can we find enlightenment?

Just as Zen says that "not doing" is what we need *to do*, it also says that to "have no goal" *is* our goal. Some take this way too literally. Not only is there nothing wrong with having the goal of attaining enlightenment or earning a black belt in martial arts, but if we are being honest, why the hell would we put ourselves through such a harrowing ordeal if we didn't have that goal?

If we've learned anything so far, at the very least we should understand that the goal is not the problem, but our attachment to the pursuit of it. And remember how I explained that the guys that preach martial arts should never be used, do so as a way to rationalize that they can't? Well, perhaps, those people who rant about not wanting enlightenment do so to rationalize why they aren't enlightened.

I'm not being harsh, just realistic. It's much easier to give up than it is to persevere. Sadly, most martial arts practitioners give up as a result of misunderstanding just what exactly enlightenment and the black belt truly mean. So next I'll take a jab at explaining it. Get it? *Jab!*

13

BLACK BELT ENLIGHTENMENT

A black belt is just a white belt that never quit.
— UNKNOWN

*The real meaning of enlightenment is to gaze
with undimmed eyes on all darkness.*
— NIKOS KAZANTZAKIS

A martial arts student went to a master and said earnestly, "I am completely devoted to studying your system. How long will it take me to master it?"

"Ten years," the teacher calmly replied.

"But I want to achieve mastery faster than that," the student anxiously replied. "I will work harder than everyone else! Practice every day, ALL DAY! How long will it take then?"

"Twenty years!" the master roared.

After they've found the right teacher, the right material, and have finally gotten on the mat and the cushion, most martial arts and Buddhist students think that the hard part is over. Most become laser-focused on their ultimate goal, which in martial arts is the coveted black belt and in Buddhism is enlightenment, and think that the harder they work the quicker they will achieve their goal. The story at the beginning of this chapter points to the fact that the more you desire something, the harder you chase it, but the more elusive it becomes.

Most students think that with greater fervor comes greater results. Well, sorry to break it to you, but rather than getting to the easiest part of the journey, what you need now is patience, as you've just started a never ending, painfully slow process of making mistakes, correcting them, and making new ones. It's a process of ego-crushing challenges, mentally taxing obstacles, bumps, bruises, and injuries … and the most gratifying thing you'll ever do! Many start, but few last.

I'm not talking about the local McDojos, which hand out black belts to five-year-olds, where, as long as you have a high enough limit on your Visa card, you are guaranteed to be promoted; where you really could learn everything they have to teach in a few months, but they string you along by teaching you a useless new kata every once and a while. (Note: A kata is a choreographed solo dance routine of "techniques."

Most systems have 10 to 15 katas required for rank promotion, with each rank having its own kata. The ridiculous thing is that you could actually learn them all in the first few months, but then there would be nothing further to learn, hence the reason they only teach you one every few months. The irony is that kata is the thing that they put the most emphasis on as a requirement for rank, and the thing you spend the majority of your time doing, yet it is completely useless for protecting yourself.)

The sad (and scary) thing is that these McDojos that fast-track rank to anyone who can afford it are extremely successful. Why? Because they make what is supposed to be an extremely hard path that few are ever able to follow seem ridiculously easy, which in turn attracts all the people that never would have made it pursuing a legitimate training. They actually exploit and strengthen the weaknesses that the martial arts are supposed to eradicate. Simply put, they give people an easy way out and then reward them for taking it. For every one Brazilian jiu jitsu black belt given, there are millions of McDojo black belts sold; make that billions…

Which begs the question, just what are we supposed to attain, how are we supposed to attain it, and why is it so different from teacher to teacher?

Most people don't realize that there is very little, if any regulation of instructors, be it competency of ability or criminal background investigation; nor is there much standardization of material taught or any consensus on what constitutes earning rank. In fact, the black belt differs so tremendously from school to school that one school's black belt could be no better than another school's white belt! Yes, it's that ridiculous! But before we discuss the differences between black belts, we need to address some misconceptions *about* the black belt.

The first and foremost issue to clear up is that most martial arts students think that the attaining of a black belt is the culmination of training, that it represents the highest level of competence. Based on this idea, they assume that its achievement is the reward for having completed one's training. Nothing could be farther from the truth. The reality is that the black belt represents the *beginning* of training, as the process of attaining it is a test of dedication and perseverance that only a few students can pass.

At the same time, the process weeds out those students who can't. As an old proverb says, "Many step on the mat, few stay." Another way of looking at it is when I am asked, "How long does it take for the average person to get a black belt?" I answer, "An average person will *never* get a black belt."

Achieving a black belt is a statement that you are not the average person, that you are one of the few who stayed, one of the few who persevered and remained completely committed through an arduous process that brought with it extreme duress. It's a statement that quitting is never an option for you and that training is a way of life rather than a part-time hobby. Putting skill level and quality of training aside, the black belt represents that you have faced your own truth and have fought the demons that would have had you quit and won. That's not the same as saying, however, that persevering in a McDojo allows you to accomplish the benefits of true training.

Before we explore what constitutes the validity of a black belt, let me share a few McDojo stories with you. I used to do regular seminars and private lessons at a school, and the owner asked me to be present for their black belt testing. (Before you start screaming, "What were you doing at a McDojo?" Remember, I make a living teaching martial arts, so if an instructor wants to bring me in to teach what he isn't capable of, I'm down with that, because it allows me to make my living as well as help make a school better.)

Anyway, I agreed, but rather than just sitting at the table like a pompous ass (not my style), I asked if I could participate in the self-defense portion of the testing. The three students testing knew me and had taken my seminars, so I figured they would be comfortable with it. My objective was to help them have a testing experience they could truly feel proud of, aside from just doing their katas.

A few weeks before the test, the students (two men in their forties and a 17-year-old girl), their instructor, and I met to discuss it. The agreed-upon format was that they would first demonstrate techniques required by their instructor in a choreographed, controlled manner, and then with me, they would each do a "freestyle," reality-based, unrehearsed portion, with me as the attacker. I would be free to do anything I wanted as an attack, and they would be able to respond with whatever defense they were spontaneously capable of. Obviously, I wasn't a fan of the rehearsed portion, but their agreement to the "live" portion with me made up for it in my eyes.

Well, things didn't go exactly as I thought they would. Without my knowledge, at some point between our meeting and the day of the test, the definition of "freestyle" changed from being live attacks with spontaneous responses to making up a routine of attacks and responses in a freestyle mix and match of anything they knew, and they would be performing their rehearsed routines with a willing partner.

Suffice to say, I was pissed off! My first impulse was to leave, as I didn't want my presence to lend any credibility to it, but since I knew these students, my gut told me that this was what the instructor wanted and not them. So I approached each one and asked if they still wanted to do the "live" portion with me as they had planned. I know some might think that it was a disrespectful move to do this against the instructor's wishes, but I was not only pissed off that the instructor would take this opportunity away from them but I genuinely cared about them and thought it unfair they couldn't have the testing they wanted, especially since they were paying for it.

The 17-year-old girl jumped at the opportunity, as did one of the men, but the other guy not only refused but did his lame rehearsed routine with the 17-year-old girl rather than with the other guy! These were the most embarrassing martial arts moments I have ever witnessed! Watching a 40-something man throwing around a 17–year-old, compliant girl as he performed his routine was pathetic. He was even taking pride in it—smiling, as the ignorant crowd clapped after every move.

After a meek attempt by the instructor to change the other two students' minds, it was time for the other two students to go. The young girl did phenomenally well! The whole audience saw the difference between what she was doing and what the guy before her did and went wild! She was tougher than the guy who wimped out, and the whole crowd knew it! The guy who did his freestyle with me was equally impressive. I came at him full steam with an array of unrehearsed attacks. Guns, knives, clubs, chokes, takedowns, punches—he handled it all very well... Well, except for one. During one punching attack, he stepped the wrong way and caught a punch to the face. The crowd freaked out as his lip exploded and blood shot everywhere.

While everyone there thought that this was a horrible moment, including the guy testing, I thought it was the best moment of the test and took the opportunity to say so. It was a moving moment as just he and I stood in the middle of the mat, the crowd around us silent.

"I know that you think this moment was a moment of failure," I said to him and the crowd, " but not only was it a moment of success, it was the best moment of today, because it was the most *real* moment of today! No altercation happens without injury. In fact, almost all altercations will start with you being injured from a sneak attack. And true success is to be able to not mentally crumble when it happens."

He seemed to perk up as I spoke, and the crowd shifted from disgust to admiration.

"You will look back at this moment and see how vital it was to your progress," I continued. "Why? Because rather than fall apart when you got hit, you pulled it together! You stayed focused and controlled. This one moment alone not only makes you worthy of your promotion, but will make others doubt theirs."

I noticed the other guy look down when I said this, but it had to be said. I needed to make clear to all present that even within the same test, there was a vast difference of integrity and character, and as a result, completely different black belts being awarded.

So what exactly gives a program and the black belt that it awards integrity? Should the amount of material in the curriculum matter? Should it be mastery of all the material taught in a minimal curriculum that ends, or mastery of some material in a large, never ending curriculum? Is it only based on skill level? Does it mean being an invincible fighter who can mop the floor with anyone? Is it perfect execution while demonstrating an exact technique in a rehearsed, choreographed routine? Or is it the ability to modify and improvise technique under realistic circumstances? Is it based completely on one's technique when compared with another's?

Or should a person's subjective issues, such as age, weight, fitness level, be factored in to the assessment of their ability?

And let's not forget their heart or spirit. One practitioner might be an amazing natural athlete for whom everything comes fairly easily. Another may have little to no dexterity or athleticism but display the kind of spirit that allows them, through sheer willpower, to fight with every ounce of blood, sweat, and tears for every tiny bit of physical progress, yet still in the end be overshadowed by the natural athlete. Who's to say which is better?

Before I answer, another story!

An old friend of mine called me one day, partly to query me and partly to complain about a practitioner with a purple belt in jiu jitsu who was opening a gym close to his karate school.

He asked me, "How is that he can open a school and teach with *only* a purple belt?"

I laughed, as I explained to him that not only did it take longer for that guy to get a purple belt than it did for him to get his black belt 25 years earlier but that while he was still teaching the same old, outdated limited curriculum from years ago, jiu jitsu was a never ending, constantly evolving training.

"Yeah," my friend countered, "but what about his level of ability?"

I laughed harder as I pointed out how most of jiu jitsu training was going live against resisting opponents, and that a jiu jitsu purple belt would wipe the mat with him!

"But that doesn't make him an instructor," he countered.

"Nor does a black belt," I shot back.

In the end he was so attached to his idea of black belt, he couldn't (though I'd say, wouldn't) accept that what you could actually do on the mat not the color of your belt is the ultimate statement of ability. To acknowledge this fact would mean that he would have to accept the inferiority of his style and his own failings as a martial artist, which in turn would undermine the validity of his black belt.

But the other point of this story is that a purple belt in jiu jitsu is a huge accomplishment, as less than 15 percent of people that start jiu jitsu ever reach it. And while a practitioner with a purple belt in jiu jitsu can surely teach, a black belt in jiu jitsu takes eight to ten years to achieve, which is, in my experience, at the very least, twice the amount of time it takes to get a black belt in most other styles.

Now, of course, time doesn't mean anything if it's wasted or filled with useless training; however, as I mentioned, with half of the training being live fighting and the other half spent on a curriculum so deep you couldn't come close to mastering it in a lifetime, it's no wonder that fewer than 1 percent of students who start jiu jitsu ever earn this prestigious level.

There are no easy answers to what mandates the criteria for defining the black belt, and ultimately there's a little bit of each one of the aforementioned issues factored in to deciding that issue, as well as who is worthy of being awarded one. I would have to say that the definition of a black belt will always be extremely different from dojo to dojo, and rather than focusing on it, we should focus on the holder and their integrity regarding it. Meaning, that the person wearing it must understand the vast differences that can be found between different black belts, and act accordingly.

Whether you have a black belt in demonstrating kata or a black sash in the gymnastic moves of wushu, be proud of it. But realize what it is and what it is not, and present it and yourself that way. Admit what you can and cannot do, and don't misrepresent what your style can and cannot do.

If you don't train techniques live, and have never been in a real-life situation, then don't say that you know what would work in one. If you compete in point sparring games of tag, don't say you're a fighter. If you do tai chi, speak of its health benefits and meditative aspects, but don't talk about self-defense. If you practice a traditional kata and ancient weapons curriculum, proudly expound on the historic and cultural traditions you're carrying on, but don't try to justify how it fits into the modern world of fighting. Make sure that you can walk your talk! Make sure that you can do on the mat what you say you can do, otherwise, that black belt of yours is just something that holds up your gi pants.

Ultimately, a black belt is really just a white belt that never quit, and the most important rank promotion is from nothing to white belt, as it signifies that you started something that most students want to achieve but never will! As the famed Buddhist teacher Suzuki once said, "Always keep your beginner's mind. In the beginner's mind, there are endless possibilities; in the expert's mind, there are few."

If the black belt is the ultimate goal of the martial artist, then the "black belt" for Buddhists would be the prestigious rank of enlightenment. The issue of enlightenment causes much of the same fervor among even the most enlightened practitioners as the black belt does in martial arts.

What is enlightenment? First, as with different styles of martial arts, different Buddhist traditions can't even agree on how it happens and what to call it, let alone describe it! Some say it's a gradual process, while others say it's sudden. Some call the experience "enlightenment" and describe it as directly experiencing emptiness, while others call it "nirvana" and describe it as experiencing the end of suffering. Confusingly, the Heart Sutra uses both words. It begins by saying, "Clearly seeing the emptiness of all the five conditions, we completely remove misfortune and pain," then ends with, "Far beyond deluded thoughts *this* is nirvana."

Now add to that all the other nifty hints that Buddhist teachings and teachers drop about enlightenment. These include, "To be attached to things is delusion, to encounter the absolute, not yet enlightenment" or

"True enlightenment is beyond both delusion and enlightenment" or the ever-frustrating "If you think you are, you're not!" Then after telling us to find enlightenment, they hit us with, "Just sitting in meditation *is* enlightenment as you already are enlightened ... you just need to discover it!" And to complicate it even further, they say that we have it all ass backwards, as we mistakenly search for this altered state called enlightenment, while enlightenment is just what *is* when we are not in another altered state!

But wait, it gets better. After confusing us, they tell us, "Enlightenment is unattainable"; we must commit to attain it! And then, after saying we must attain it, we are told that the Buddha way is to study the "self," but to study the "self" is to *forget* the "self" and that forgetting the "self" *is* enlightenment!

My experience has been that all of the above are right! Am I saying I am enlightened? I can't, because if I do, I'm not! But seriously, what I can say is that I have had what I call enlightened moments, and as I have progressed in my practice, I have been able to string more and more of these moments together more frequently and for longer durations.

An example I often use with both martial arts and Buddhism is to liken training and practice to walking through a mist. You barely feel it when you're walking through it, but after a while you realize you're soaking wet! In much of our training and practice, we don't realize how we are being affected, thinking we're not getting it at all, then we are suddenly surprised in a random moment by how much we *are* getting it! (Or is it getting us?) These types of random moments are our first glimpses of enlightenment, but before going further in this discussion, I think it's important to define enlightenment.

As I mentioned earlier, many students misunderstand it as an altered spiritual state. First, let me go on the record and state that I hate the word "spiritual," as it fosters this idea that there is an experience other than now, as though there were some type of escape from what we are experiencing that urges us to find it and use it. But it's just this quest that sends practitioners on a wild goose chase through their own imaginations, and the longer they're chasing this idea, the farther away they get from the truth, and the harder it becomes to find their way back to it.

Does this mean that there aren't any moments in meditative practice where we experience incredible states of calmness, joy, equanimity, or bliss? Of course not. But the teachings tell us that they are just temporary moments that won't last, and that we shouldn't try to stay there or chase them.

So if enlightenment isn't an altered state, what is it? First we need to understand that the word enlightenment is an English translation. In the Buddha's teaching, the word used is "awakening," which is also defined as "to see clearly" or to "come to an understanding."

So with this in mind, I define enlightenment as a process of seeing clearly the dependent origination and interconnectedness of conditioned experience, of having an unconditional acceptance of the present that is free from attachment to our conditioned, fixed ideas and our harmful, impulsive, reactive behavior. It is to not be attached to, and living through, a construct of self; to be present in the moment without any additions, neither pursuing or avoiding anything. It involves using the intrinsic wisdom we come to understand through these experiences and turning them into skillful actions. In short, rather than enlightenment being something we find, enlightenment is something we *do*. And it's very important to note that like a lotus rising from the mud, enlightened moments are often found rising out of the most deluded situations.

The teachings tell us of the four mindsets that Buddhism identifies as best reflecting an enlightened mindset leading to enlightened actions. These are:

- Loving-kindness
- Compassion
- Sympathetic Joy
- Equanimity

Because words fall short of being able to describe enlightened experience, I've found that investigating and keeping an awareness of these four mindsets and their accompanying actions are extremely helpful in understanding enlightened experience. But remember, always be clear about the intention behind them. All four of these states have what's called a near enemy, which can seem like one of the four enlightened mind states, but because of the unhealthy intention behind them aren't.

We see a similar experience in the martial arts as well. As I've already mentioned, the typical modus operandi in a McDojo is to exploit a student's desire to achieve his or her goals by easily rewarding it based on fabrication. This is done by the following means: giving students positions in the hierarchy based on their subservience (and check writing); awarding ridiculously frequent stripes on their belts between ranks; having an insane number of different ranks, with lightning-quick promotion from one rank to another (again mostly for check writing ability); forcing lower ranking students to be subservient to higher ranking ones; mandating unearned respect; and not only awarding the black belt in an insanely short period of time but for a trivial amount of almost useless material.

In this type of program, we find people who think they have met their goals of increasing their self-esteem and becoming more confident, but sadly are only confusing their experience of this new "pride" with its near enemy, arrogance. So with this in mind, let's look at the four near enemies of Buddhism:

- Attachment
- Pity
- Selfish Exhilaration
- Indifference

The near enemies are all rooted in clinging and aversion, pursuing and avoiding, which are the basis for suffering. What makes identifying them so difficult is that they are nearly identical experiences to those of the enlightenment mindsets, and while in the midst of them, the seemingly healthy experience inhibits our ability to clearly see the harmful intention behind it. Due to the experiences being so similar, we need to examine the differences between them to learn how to recognize the differences.

Loving-kindness is defined by selfless, unconditional *giving*, while attachment, which can feel like love, is defined by *taking* and is rooted in our selfish desire, dependent on our conditions being met.

Compassion is the ability to understand another's suffering as our own and view their suffering as *our* problem, while pity stems from disconnection, viewing another's suffering as only *their* problem and being motivated to help only by the self-satisfaction of doing so.

Sympathetic joy is defined by being happy for another's happiness, while selfish exhilaration is to attach to another's happiness for our own gratification.

Equanimity is characterized by being able to be fearlessly balanced between the extremes of any situation, no matter what it may be. We can be with it, care deeply, but have a nonattached awareness of the way things are that is free from pursuing or avoiding, while indifference is a state of fearful detachment from the way things are and a sense of not caring, which is mistaken for balance but is really a state of aversion.

Once in a private session with Noah, I was talking (or probably bragging) about how I had found equanimity in a particular situation, and he laughed, "I think you just don't give a fuck!" I might have felt like I did, but he could see that I didn't, and his sudden punch-in-the-face remark knocked some sense into me. It made me stop and take a deeper look at the experience, and it was then that I realized he was right! Equanimity is to *let go* of the way we want things to be, while indifference is to *hold on* to the way we want things to be, and my not giving a fuck was exactly my way of doing this.

All that being said, like the black belt, enlightenment has as many different definitions as it does practitioner experiences, and perhaps there is a bit of truth to each one. So just like we should look at the individual black belt holder and how they represent it, more important than what people *say* about enlightenment is how they *do* enlightenment. So if we are lucky enough not to suffer, then perhaps we're lucky enough! Isn't that enlightening!

So, now, having ranted at some length about how attaining a black belt or finding enlightenment is *not* the end to our training and practice, it just doesn't seem right to have the book end with talking about just that. In fact, it's hard to write an ending to a subject that never truly ends, so the ending I feel is most appropriate for the book is to talk about how training and practice continue and *how* we continue to train and practice.

There is an old saying in the martial arts: "Every fighter has a winning fight plan until they get punched in the face!" And I say, "Every Buddhist is enlightened until they get hit with reality!" And that's just it, you can't win a fight until you are in it and have to fight back, and you can't be skillful until it's put to a reality test!

The fact is that what we *must* do continually is *fail*, and our greatest success is to clearly see that failure. The only way to get better at jiu jitsu is to lose, to constantly roll with people better than you who can expose your vulnerabilities and weaknesses. Many times in martial arts training, practitioners stop in the middle of trying to apply a technique, as they feel they should start over after it doesn't go as planned. But this is a huge training mistake, as it causes them to miss the most important part of the lesson, which is that failure is the most relevant truth each of us can face: more important than knowing *what* to do is being able to do *something*, when what you know doesn't work, that we are training and practicing not to get *good* at what we *think* will work, but to get *real* when it *doesn't*.

With these sentiments in mind, we can understand that our training and practice are a never-ending, continuing process of making mistakes and fixing them. A Zen master once said, "Life is one continuous mistake" and another said, "You are perfect as you are; you just need some improvement."

Don't Believe a
Stinkin' Word of This!

Zen says words can't explain the "Zen experience"—that studying or practicing Zen does not involve thinking about what you know about Zen, and that being stuck in your ideas about Zen makes you "stink" of Zen. Now that I am typing the last bit of this book, I know that if I am lucky enough to get it published, and even luckier to have someone read it, by the time it gets into someone's hands, it will be nothing but words that fall way short of explaining the "Jeff experience."

To my surprise, writing this book taught me much about myself and the process of practice, as writing itself became a practice of sorts. When I started writing this, I was an investigator and martial arts school owner, extremely busy with work, my own martial arts training, and attending meditation sessions and dharma talks. If and when I wrote, it was for very brief time periods, which often had long timeframes of inactivity in between them. What became frustrating was that each time that I went back to writing after an extended break, I found that what I had written, while I liked it for what it said, and thought others might find it helpful, was no longer pertinent to my practice. The person who had written it no longer existed! The opinions stated had changed. The practice I was doing was different.

When I put something to the page I wanted it to be authentic, and while it was at the time, it would never be for long, as truth is constantly changing, and we are constantly evolving, and rather than the truth freeing us, we get stuck when we try to hold onto it. Rather than accepting this, I would find myself either deleting what I had written entirely, or rewriting it to reflect my current place in practice. But no matter how often I did this, and did it again, and again, and again, from the moment I finished writing something, it seemed to become almost instantly irrelevant!

I finally had to learn to write and not look back, and this is my advice to you on how you should read it as well. I hope that you found that it was worth reading, even if the result was that you hated it and that it showed you exactly how you *don't* want your training or practice to be (which I would think would be the most worthwhile result), but now that you have read it, don't look back. Keep moving forward and have a new experience.

> A master had only one successor. He called this student into his room and said, "I am getting old, and you are my chosen one to carry forward the teaching. I present to you this book. It is extremely valuable as it's been passed down from master to master for generations, and all of them, including myself, have added our own comments of understanding to it."
>
> "If it is such an important book to you," the student said, "you should keep it. I received the teachings without it, and I don't need it." The master insisted that the student take it and thrust it into his hands, at which the student instantly threw it in the fire next to them!
>
> "What are you doing?" The master yelled.
>
> "What are you saying?" The student screamed back.

The truth and our own authenticity are not found in stagnation but in the shifting and changing of circumstance. Whether it's Buddhist or martial arts practice, we must not believe in it; we must doubt it. It's this doubting that forces us to let go and move forward. Belief closes our minds in one place, while doubt opens them to a world of possibility.

Always remember that a Zen master described life as "one continuous mistake." The best way to get better at jiu jitsu is to tap out, as losing helps you see what you need to work on and improve. In Buddhist practice, failure is the catalyst for the doubt we need to motivate ourselves to improve the application of our practice.

So now that you're done reading this, give it away, put it in your pile of books, and forget about it or burn it! But whatever you do, please doubt every stinkin' word of it, because there's no doubt that I sure do!

The Way of the Fighting Buddha

Teachers

- Never follow blindly. Your teacher should have to earn your respect and loyalty.
- Sometimes the best teacher teaches you to recognize what not to do.
- A great teacher's goal is to make their student better than themselves.

Martial Arts

- Identify your training goals.
- Be sure the training you've chosen supports your goals.
- Test concepts under realistic circumstances to determine if they have realistic application.
- Don't train to get good; train to get real.
- Ninety-nine percent of the work is just showing up! Get on the mat and cushion no matter what—especially when you least want to.
- Train like today is that one day that you'll need to use your training.
- How long does it take for the average person to get a black belt? The *average* person *doesn't* get a black belt.
- A black belt is just a white belt that never quit.

Buddhism

- Create the discipline to be disciplined.
- Practice each day like everything that *can* go wrong *will*.
- Every situation is an opportunity to transform oneself.
- Enlightenment is not an altered state; it's the waking up from an altered state.
- Reality is always different from what we think it is.
- Sometimes the answer is that you're asking the wrong question.
- Be mindful of when you're not.
- Do not doing.
- Doubt everything.

Suggested Reading List

While I have referenced and utilized Buddhist sutras, koans, philosophy, and stories in the text as the vehicles to make my points, this is based on my personal understanding and interpretation in regard to my own experiences and practice. I have merely scratched the surface of these great teachings. For the reader who wishes to learn more on these subjects, I suggest the following reading:

Batchelor, Stephen. *Buddhism Without Beliefs*. New York: Penguin, 1998.

_____. *The Faith to Doubt: Glimpses of Buddhist Uncertainty*. Berkeley: Counter Point Press, 2015.

_____. *Confessions of a Buddhist Atheist*. New York: Spiegel & Grau, 2010.

_____. *Buddhism: Rethinking the Dharma for a Secular Age.* New Haven: Yale University Press, 2015.

_____. *Living with the Devil: A Meditation on Good and Evil*. New York: Penguin, 2005.

Beck, Charlotte. *Every Day Zen: Love and Work.* San Francisco: HarperCollins, 1989.

_____. *Nothing Special: Living Zen*. San Francisco: HarperCollins, 1993.

Brunnholzl, Karl. *The Heart Attack Sutra: A New Commentary on the Heart Sutra*. Boston: Snow Lion, 2012.

Glassman, Bernie and Rick Fields. *Instructions to the Cook: A Zen Master's Lessons in Living a Life That Matters.* Boston: Shambhala Publications, 1996.

Hartman, Blanche. *Seeds for a Boundless Life: Zen Teachings From the Heart.* Boston: Shambhala Publications, 2015.

Ford, James, Blacker, Melissa. *The Book of MU: Essential Writings On Zen's Most Important Koan.* Boston: Wisdom Publications, 2011.

Gyatso, Kelsang. *The Bodhisattva Vow: A Practical Guide for Helping Others.* New York: Tharpa Publications, 1991.

Kapleau, Philip. *The Three Pillars of Zen: Teaching, Practice, and Enlightenment.* New York: Anchor Books, 1965.

Kornfield, Jack. Bringing *Home the Dharma. Awakening Right Where You Are.* Boston: Shambhala, 2011.

Loori, Daido John. *Cave of Tigers: The Living Zen Practice of Dharma Combat.* New York: Weatherhill, 2000.

Levine, Noah. *Against the Stream: A Buddhist Manual for Spiritual Revolutionaries.* New York: HarperCollins, 2009.

———. *The Heart of the Revolution: The Buddha's Radical Teachings of Forgiveness, Compassion, and Kindness.* New York: HarperCollins, 2011.

Nichtern, Ethan. One *City: A Declaration of Interdependence.* Boston: Wisdom Publications, 2007.

———. *The Road Home: A Contemporary Exploration of the Buddhist Path.* New York: North Point Press, 2015.

Nichtern, David. *Awakening from the Daydream: Reimagining the Buddha's Wheel of Life.* Boston: Wisdom Publications, 2016.

Soho, Takuan and William Scott Wilson. *The Unfettered Mind: Writings of the Zen Master to the Sword Master.* Tokyo: Kodansha International, 1986.

Suzuki, Shunryu. *Zen Mind, Beginners Mind: Informal Talks on Zen Meditation and Practice.* New York: Weatherhill, 1970.

———. *Always So: Practicing the True Spirit of Zen.* New York: HarperCollins, 2002.

Wick, Shishin Gerry. *The book of Equanimity: Illuminating Classic Zen Koans.* Boston: Wisdom Publications, 2005.

Wallace, B. Alan. *Tibetan Buddhism From the Ground Up: A Practical Approach for Modern Life.* Boston: Wisdom Publications, 1993.

Warner, Brad. *Don't be a Jerk: And Other Practical Advice from Dogen, Japan's Greatest Zen Master.* Navato: New World Library, 2016.

_____. *Sit Down and Shut Up: Punk Rock Commentaries on Buddha, God, Sex, Death, and Dogen's Treasury of the Right Dharma Eye*. Navato: New World Library, 2007

Yamamoto, Tsunetomo, Minoru Tanaka, and Justin F. Stone. *Bushido: Way of the Samurai*. New York: Square One Publishers, 2001.

Acknowledgments

First and foremost, I need to thank my wife, Linda. While I desperately need Buddhist practice just to make me bearable, she is a Buddha without even trying! Her natural and effortless ability to be kind and compassionate are traits that all of us hard-working Buddhists aspire to but will never attain, no matter how hard we try! I'm grateful that she has stuck around for 23 years to see me finally start winning some battles against Mara!

Thank you to all my family and friends for your support, as well as all the teachers and training partners I've had over the years, both good and bad! You've all taught me something that has played a part in this book!

Finally, thank you to Findhorn Press and my editors, Sabine Weeke and Nicky Leach, for believing in my work and taking a mess of a manuscript and turning it into a presentable book!

About the Author

Photo: © Alix Petricek

Jeff Eisenberg was born in Irvington, New Jersey in 1964. He started training in the martial arts as a child and has been training consistently for over 45 years. He is a Grand Master level martial arts instructor, with over 30 years of teaching experience, and ran his own dojo for almost 15 years.

Always priding himself on being a student, he has repeatedly taken off his black belt to put on a white belt and pursue training in a new style. This has taken him on an extensive journey through the martial arts of judo, karate, muay Thai, kali, escrima, hapkido, aikido, and Japanese jiu jitsu. His current martial arts pursuit is Brazilian jiu jitsu, in which he's been training for the last eight years. He is also a certified protection specialist and defensive tactics instructor and has worked as a bodyguard and investigator.

He was first introduced to meditation through his martial arts training, and this introduction began his lifelong interest in mental discipline and Eastern philosophy, particularly Buddhism, which he has been practicing for most of his adult life.

Jeff currently lives with his wife, Linda, and a bunch of cats, across the street from the beach at the Jersey Shore. For more information and contact visit his website: *fightingbuddhadojo.com*

FINDHORN PRESS

Life-Changing Books

Consult our catalogue online
(with secure order facility) on
www.findhornpress.com

For information on the Findhorn Foundation:
www.findhorn.org

green press
INITIATIVE

Findhorn Press is committed to preserving ancient forests and natural resources. We elected to print this title on 30% post consumer recycled paper, processed chlorine free. As a result, for this printing, we have saved:

9 Trees (40' tall and 6-8" diameter)
4 Million BTUs of Total Energy
778 Pounds of Greenhouse Gases
4,215 Gallons of Wastewater
282 Pounds of Solid Waste

Findhorn Press made this paper choice because our printer, Thomson-Shore, Inc., is a member of Green Press Initiative, a nonprofit program dedicated to supporting authors, publishers, and suppliers in their efforts to reduce their use of fiber obtained from endangered forests.

For more information, visit www.greenpressinitiative.org

Environmental impact estimates were made using the Environmental Defense Paper Calculator. For more information visit: www.papercalculator.org.

FSC
www.fsc.org

MIX
Paper from responsible sources
FSC® C013483